MAKING SAMPLERS

Detail of a sampler embroidered in 1784
(see page 50)

Overleaf: English Berlin woolwork panel for a firescreen, 1850s

THE

EMBROIDERERS' GUILD

PRACTICAL LIBRARY

·

MAKING
SAMPLERS

David & Charles

Co-ordinated by Margaret Rivers

Photography by Dudley Moss and Julia Hedgecoe (see Acknowledgements)

A DAVID & CHARLES BOOK

First published 1993
Reprinted 1994

A catalogue record for this book is available from the British Library.

ISBN 0 7153 9991 8

Typeset by ABM Typographics Ltd, Hull
and printed in Italy by Milanostampa SpA
for David & Charles
Brunel House Newton Abbot Devon

CONTENTS

Detail of clothed boxer figures from a band sampler worked in England in the seventeenth century

INTRODUCTION

Samplers are and always have been one of the most popular forms of embroidery. Today, many embroiderers enjoy creating a decorative sampler to record an important family event, while people from all walks of life are intrigued by the information captured in stitch by sampler makers of centuries past. Understanding samplers is not quite so simple as reading the pages of a book, but the information preserved within these embroideries can be deciphered and released to become part of the story of the women and children who made them.

The Embroiderers' Guild Collection contains samplers which illustrate almost four hundred years of sampler making in Britain. A selection of these historic designs is presented in this book alongside the modern samplers they have inspired contemporary embroiderers to create. These modern sampler projects, which appear in this book with full instructions, charts and patterns, are designed to appeal to embroiderers of all levels of experience. Some are quite challenging, but others can be attempted by complete beginners. Each of the twenty new projects has its own special charm and today's embroiderer can read about the historical background of the original before embarking on the contemporary version it has inspired.

The word 'sampler' derives from the Latin word *exemplum* meaning pattern or model. The earliest embroidered samplers were produced as technical trial pieces and used as reference works of stitches and designs. The earliest surviving dated sampler, stitched by Jane Bostocke in 1598, is preserved in the Victoria and Albert Museum in London. A now-famous inventory of 1502 which itemises the purchases made for Elizabeth, wife of Henry VII, is the earliest documentary evidence of the existence of samplers in Britain. This list includes 'an elne of lynnyn cloth for a sampler for the Quene viij d'. There are other sixteenth-century documents which mention or list samplers, and it is a mark of their value that they were often itemised in inventories and bequeathed by will.

A domestic art

Embroidery flourished as a domestic art in sixteenth-century Britain, when textiles were particularly important in providing warmth, comfort and decoration. A period of peace and increasing affluence allowed the population to concentrate on domestic concerns and the decorative arts. After the dissolution of the monasteries and the reformation of the Church, formal and ceremonial costumes and sumptuous civic furnishings were professionally embroidered. Skilled amateurs made embroidered costume pieces and furnishings for their homes. In the larger and more affluent households domestic embroiderers (family members and servants) may well have been assisted in their task by an itinerant or resident embroiderer engaged for the purpose.

Embroiderers looked to several sources for their designs: those who could afford it might have employed a professional to draft one, or they could copy or 'prick and pounce' motifs themselves from printed patterns and illustrations in books. Most chose to copy their designs from existing embroideries, as this was the most widely available option. The first printed embroidery pattern book was published in Germany in 1524 and although a series of pattern books for lace, needlework and embroidery followed, they probably remained relatively rare for some time. Consequently the sampler was not made redundant, and continued to be relied on by many embroiderers as a medium for recording designs for future use, as well as a practice ground for their skills.

Random spot samplers

The Embroiderers' Guild's earliest sampler (opposite) belongs to a distinctive group of embroideries which are usually referred to as spot, or random spot samplers. These names

reflect the arrangement of individual motifs on the ground fabric. Surviving examples tend to date from the early-seventeenth century when they were functional rather than decorative. An embroiderer would try out new stitches on her sampler, and use it to record motifs and patterns for future reference. Early samplers took a comparatively squat rectangular shape, becoming longer and narrower as the seventeenth century progressed. The sampler shown above is actually a fragment of a larger embroidery. When not being used, the sampler would have been rolled and stored in a workbox.

The predominantly geometric motifs on this sampler are reminiscent of Tudor strapwork patterns and even the layout of sixteenth-century knot gardens. This reminds us that embroidery was not produced in a vacuum, but subject to changing fashions and styles of the time. The richly encrusted, raised appearance of the motifs is achieved through the use of silk and metal threads. Linen ground fabrics, silk and metal threads were characteristically employed to work these early samplers. Such sumptuous embroidery could very well have been used to decorate small purses and pin-

Fragment of an English spot sampler, early-seventeenth century

cushions; and similar designs might have been destined for clothes. The embroiderer of this sampler has left each motif incomplete, presumably deliberately to show how the stitches are built up. Some spot samplers contain individual bird, beast, plant and flower designs which were also extremely popular during the late-sixteenth and early-seventeenth centuries.

Costume pieces

These designs can be seen on actual costume and furnishing pieces of the period. Look at the panel illustrated on the following page; it is worked with fine silks and metal threads in detached needlelace, plaited braid and chain stitches which give the design a strong three-dimensional element. Although the coiling framework does not appear on samplers, the motifs themselves – the flower heads, bird and insects – can be found on some samplers, and can certainly be traced to printed patterns. This panel was probably cut down from a coif (woman's cap).

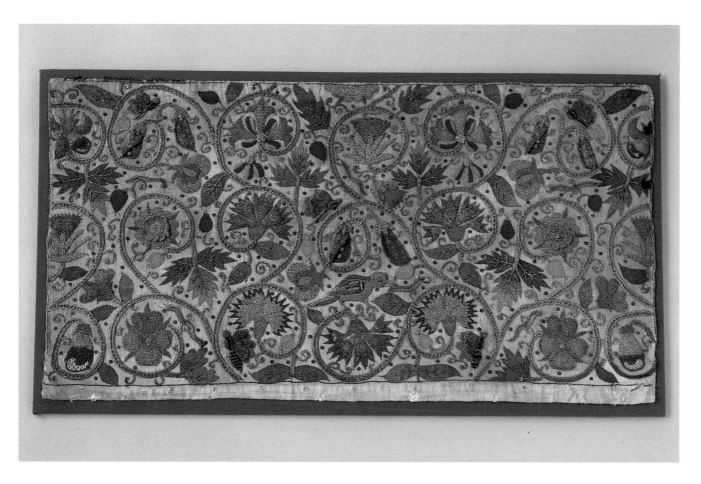

Panel possibly from a coif made in England in the early-seventeenth century

Band samplers

As the seventeenth century progressed, samplers lengthened into long, narrow strips of linen cut from a loom width of cloth – hence the selvedge found at the top and bottom of many of them. The approximate average dimensions of this type of seventeenth-century sampler were between 60–90cm (2–3ft) in length and 13–25cm (5–10in) in width. They provided substantial pieces of cloth on which an embroiderer could practise and demonstrate her stitchcraft.

The lengthening of the sampler was not the only change to occur in the seventeenth century. A second distinctive development was that the embroidered patterns were now stitched as horizontal bands across the full, but narrow, width of the linen. It was this that led to the embroideries being called band samplers. The change in layout was not sudden and dramatic: spot samplers were still stitched during the early decades of the 1600s and some embroiderers throughout the century continued to reserve a section of their band samplers to stitch individual motifs.

A variety of stitch techniques can be found on band samplers including examples of cut and drawn work, needlelace and lacis worked in white linen threads. Some samplers were devoted to these and whitework embroidery alone. Many band samplers combined embroidery worked in coloured silk threads with lace and whitework techniques. Usually only a relatively short length of the linen ground was reserved for the latter, leaving the coloured embroidery to dominate. Although metal thread was often a feature of spot motifs it was rarely used to embroider band patterns.

Looking at a collection of nineteenth-century samplers it is likely that a very limited range of stitches was used, and often not very well. This was certainly not the case with samplers embroidered in the 1600s. Their range of techniques has already been mentioned; the coloured patterns also employed a variety of stitches. *The Needle's Excellency*, one of the most popular embroidery pattern books published in England in the seventeenth century, was prefaced by a poem by John Taylor which listed an ex-

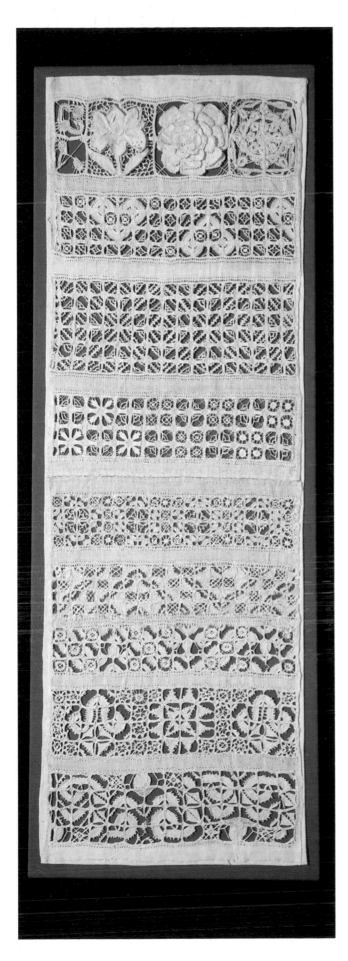

tensive range of the contemporary embroidery techniques and stitches:

> For Tent-worke, Rais'd-worke, Laid-worke,
>   Frost-worke, Net-worke,
> Most curious Purles, or rare Italian cutworke
> Fine Ferne-stitch, Finny-stitch, New-stitch and
>   Chain-stitch
> Braue Bred-stitch, Fisher-stitch, Irish-stitch and
>   Queen-stitch
> The Spanish-stitch, Rosemary-stitch, and
>   Mouse-stitch
> The smarting Whip-stitch, Back-stitch and the
>   Crosse-stitch,
> All these are good and we must allow
> And these are everywhere in practise now.

Not every seventeenth-century band sampler would use all or even half this number of stitches; but those which were used were handled with considerable skill, making technical excellence a feature of many surviving embroideries.

A change in function

The difference between spot and band samplers was not simply in the layout of the motifs and patterns embroidered upon them: during the course of the seventeenth century the *function* of the sampler changed too. The sampler moved from being a working tool, a reference work of stitch and design, to being one of a series of technical exercises completed by young girls as part of their needlework education. A child would begin the curriculum by stitching one or more band samplers in coloured embroidery, and follow these with similar sampler exercises in cutwork, needlelace and general whitework embroidery.

After sampler making the young embroiderer would progress to a series of decorative items (tent-stitched pictures, beadwork objects, embroidered boxes and mirror frames) which allowed her to try new techniques and demonstrate her proficiency in those already acquired. The mirror frame or box decorated with three-dimensional raised work was the ultimate virtuoso piece and culmination of a girl's needlework education. A fine example of this final stage survives in the Embroiderers' Guild

Collection. The illustration (right) shows the lid of this box, depicting a series of embroidered scenes which together tell the story of David and Bathsheba, one of the Old Testament Bible stories which were popular with the young embroiderers. As you can see this panel is particularly well drawn and was probably professionally designed. Our embroiderer could well have purchased this satin panel ready drawn.

Contemporary embroiderers are often amazed, and deflated, by the extreme youth of their seventeenth-century predecessors. Very usefully for us, these earlier embroiderers took to signing their work, and recording on it not only the date when the embroidery was made but their age at the time of completion. Such information tells us that girls as young as eight or nine years of age were capable of completing their first samplers, and could reach the stage of decorating a box with embroidery by the time they were twelve years old.

During the early years of the 1700s the long narrow sampler shortened into a squat rectangle of cloth. The arrangement of patterns and motifs changed too; and new decorative devices were added. Eventually the type of embroidery which most people think of as a typical sampler emerged: that is, one with a strong pictorial emphasis, or central focal point. In such samplers, motifs, pious verse, and stitched alphabets were increasingly surrounded by decorative embroidered borders. These borders are good evidence that eighteenth-century embroiderers regarded their samplers as being decorative as well as, or even rather than, functional embroideries.

An educational exercise

As we have seen, early samplers were valuable tools for teaching technical skills. The addition of alphabets, numerals, and the occasional recording of teachers and school names have all encouraged us to see the sampler as a schoolroom product and aid. Exactly what the embroidered sampler was used to teach, and how successfully, is worth thought. As the eighteenth century passed into the nineteenth, the number of stitches found on samplers declined dramatically until cross stitch reigned alone. Surely these simple samplers could not claim to teach embroidery? Because stitched alphabets and numerals were often included on the samplers, there is a theory that they were

Box lid in raised work from England, circa 1650–1675

used to teach literacy and numeracy. Many seventeenth- and eighteenth-century samplers are found embroidered with misformed letters, words misspelt and run together, suggesting that the makers had not yet grasped the meaning of the letters which they stitched. It is possible that stitched alphabets provided girls with symbols for marking and identifying textiles, although a decorative device such as a crown or coronet served just as well for this purpose.

Pious and moralising verse became a feature of eighteenth- and nineteenth-century samplers. The ability to read was obviously necessary to make the message effective. The content of sampler verse suggests that young people in earlier centuries were rarely cossetted from worldly concerns. Eighteenth-century samplers featured verses on morality and death, and frequently described the need to lead a useful and virtuous Christian life, coupled with an acceptance that it would probably be a short one. Many of the stitched verses were not original compositions but were taken from the work of other authors – in particular Dr Isaac Watts and the hymns written by Phillip Dodderidge and John Wesley. Dr Watts believed that 'what is learned in verse is longer retained in memory and recollected'. No doubt the laborious effort involved in embroidering these verses would have ensured that their sentiments were known by heart.

Map samplers are frequently associated with schoolroom learning, though it is worth pondering how much geography in relation to embroidery would have been learnt in making a map sampler. Some of the maps were hand drawn by the young pupils but from the 1780s even this effort was removed when commercially printed maps for embroiderers became available. Embroidered map samplers were usually highly decorative objects garlanded with flowers and sprinkled with ornaments.

During the eighteenth century other equally distinctive sampler forms appeared which did have a functional value, and were useful in teaching and demonstrating needlework skills. One of these, the darning sampler, appeared in Britain late in the eighteenth century. A very fine and decorative example is shown on page 59 of this book. Patterned darns in silk threads have been used to repair slits in the ground fabrics; and the same techniques have been employed to create multi-coloured floral motifs. It is a true virtuoso piece. Samplers like this may have been the work of professional embroiderers, perhaps teachers who presented the pieces as evidence of their qualifications.

Hollie point
Hollie point samplers were made for a limited period during the 1720s and 1730s. Hollie point, which was used as a decorative insertion in baby clothes, is a closely worked needlelace technique which leaves holes in the rows of looped stitches to create motifs, patterns and inscriptions. Also known as 'holy' point or stitch, it could be that the name derives from the method of using holes to create patterns; another theory is that this name reflects the religious bias of many of the motifs, or the belief that this needlelace was once worked in convents.

An established format
Sampler making continued into and throughout the nineteenth century. Pictorial and verse samplers remained popular. As with samplers stitched in earlier centuries, many of those made in the 1800s reflected fashionable designs and styles of the times. Berlin woolwork embroidery, a technique using woollen yarns on canvas, developed into a major obsession with amateur embroiderers during the early and middle part of the nineteenth century. The influence of this needlework became clearly apparent in the motifs and techniques used in decorative sampler making. Tent and cross stitches, simple to do, were the technical mainstay of Berlin woolwork embroidery. Cross stitch soon became the dominant and often the only stitch used in nineteenth-century decorative samplers.

The layout of these embroidereries followed the format established in the eighteenth century, and which is now seen as the traditional sampler design. Within the guidelines of this tradition embroiderers selected and arranged their motifs and verse with some individuality. However, in the late-nineteenth century very definite design rules were described by the authors S.F.A. Caulfield and Blanche C. Saward. In 1882 they published the *Dictionary of Needlework,* a treasure trove of information, advice and guidance for the Victorian embroiderer. The two women defined two types of sampler: a decorative embroidery, and a functional piece, and gave instructions for making

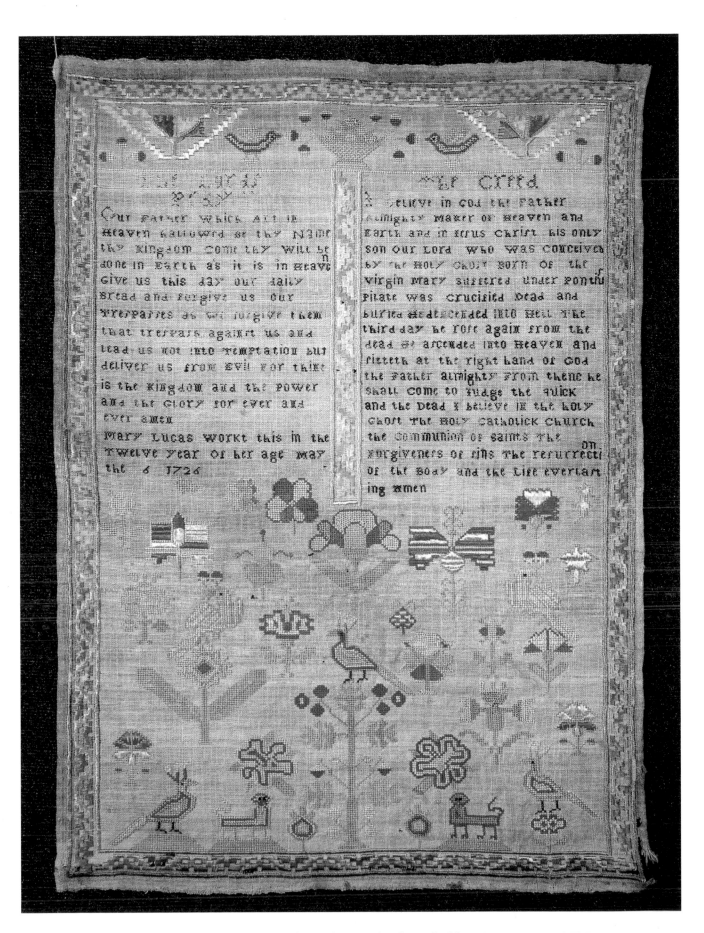

The Lord's Prayer and the Creed sampler, England, worked by Mary Lucas in 1726

both types. According to them, decorative samplers should be 45cm (18in) wide by 50cm (20in) long, and the main body of the embroidery should be enclosed by a border filled with a 'conventional scroll pattern in shades of several colours and in tent stitch'. They instructed that the sampler should be divided into three sections and decorated as follows: the top section should carry a figure design (Caulfield and Saward suggested the Adam and Eve motif), the middle ground should be occupied by a stitched alphabet in capital letters, and the base area should be filled with an 'appropriate verse', the name of the worker and the date. With variations in layout this exactly describes the content of many surviving nineteenth-century decorative samplers.

Berlin-work samplers provided a colourful, richly patterned deviant from this traditional form. Berlin samplers were usually long narrow strips of canvas backed with a vividly coloured silk or cotton lining, which was longer than the canvas itself, and into which the sampler could be rolled for protection and storage. The variety of patterns, embroidery materials (wool, silk, ribbon, beads) and techniques is usually more extensive than anything found on an average piece of Berlin-work embroidery stitched by an enthusiastic, but limited amateur embroiderer. This would almost certainly be in woollen tent and cross stitch embroidery copied from a printed mass-produced chart. The suggestion is that like spot samplers of the sixteenth and seventeenth centuries, Berlin woolwork samplers were produced and used by professional embroiderers as design and stitch reference works. Perhaps they were brought out to show the range of possibilities to potential customers. These embroideries occupy only a brief period in the history of samplers. They were stitched in the middle decades of the nineteenth century when the Berlin woolwork craze was at its peak.

The second type of sampler described by Caulfield and Saward was a purely functional piece of needlework which they called the marking sampler. Characterised by stitched alphabets, with the addition of numerals and devices such as crowns and coronets intended as identification marks for costume and furnishings, marking devices were not a new element in samplers. The production of these practical embroideries was boosted during the nine-teenth century when access to education was extended through the growth of charity and church-funded schools. Eventually, legislation enforced school attendance at elementary level. Teaching practical skills to the poor and working classes was an important part of the curriculum and resulted in a great number of alphabets, darning and plain sewing samplers. In making these samplers it was hoped that girls (and in some institutions, boys) would acquire useful skills for future use in their own homes, or domestic service in other people's houses.

A compulsory skill

In 1862 the government made functional needlework a compulsory subject for girls in elementary education and gave a financial reward to each child who reached a required standard. There was no deviation from the rules, and creativity was not encouraged. Two marking samplers in the Embroiderers' Guild Collection show how the same exercises were taught in one particular school between 1844 and 1851. The only real touch of individuality on marking samplers of that time was in the choice of verse to be stitched.

Plain sewing samplers were often mounted on the pages of a book, which as they were turned marked the child's progress through the curriculum. An early example in the Embroiderers' Guild Collection was completed at the British School in September 1827 by Ann Craddock. The now fragile paper pages preserve examples of Ann's work showing her abilities in hemming, pin-tucking, darning, making buttonholes and thread-covered buttons. The book also includes a small marking sampler worked in red silk thread on a coarse linen canvas.

The practice of amassing a collection of samplers for a teacher or examiner's scrutiny was maintained during the late-nineteenth century, and continued well into the twentieth century. As well as those studying to be teachers, young women training for careers in industry and commerce produced samplers and pieces of needlework as evidence of their skill. The object of plain sewing is to be practical rather than pretty, but a considerable number of the sample pieces produced at this time have great charm.

Student work from the late 1800s onwards reflects a deep admiration for historic masterpieces which were taken as models of excellence and meticulously copied. Although some nineteenth-century amateurs may have taken samplers into the doldrums, those who trained for a qualification in needlework were expected to achieve a high level of technical excellence. The Royal School of Art Needlework was established in 1872 to supply 'suitable employment for Gentlewomen and restoring Ornamental Needlework to the high place it once held among the decorative arts'. By the early twentieth century the Royal School of Needlework (having dropped Art from the title) was producing some highly accomplished embroiderers. Students at the RSN were tutored in traditional and difficult techniques such as metal thread embroidery, which was and still is in demand for ceremonial costumes and furnishings. Students at the RSN have often used the sampler form to practice and demonstrate their abilities. In 1910 Katherine Helena Powell used the sampler form to exhibit her skills when sitting a City and Guilds examination. The illustration clearly shows Katherine Powell's proficiency with metal thread techniques, and her work attracted a commendation from the examiners.

Adventurous work
For much of the early twentieth century embroiderers esteemed technical perfection above original design and individual creativity. The move towards more adventurous and expressive work did not take off until the 1930s and only really gathered momentum in the postwar years. Today many embroiderers are noted for their highly individual and adventurous work. With them the sampler has gone back to being a working tool, a trial piece rather than something intended for display. The experiments which these embroiderers carry out with their materials, machines and ideas are our true contemporary samplers.

Metal-thread sampler worked by Katherine Powell in England in 1910

FLOWERS FROM THE SEVENTEENTH CENTURY

A band sampler to demonstrate skill

Some extremely rich embroideries were stitched during the seventeenth century, making it a particularly interesting period for today's embroiderer to study. Who could fail to be captivated by the coiling patterns of plants and flowers, and the bird, beast and insect motifs scattered across fine linen or enthusiastically squeezed in to fill a gap, whether they relate to the main design or not?

The use of fine materials and technical skill are the hallmarks of seventeenth-century band samplers like the one shown opposite, which was made by someone with the initials K.C. (look for these initials below the pink and blue letters). Band samplers are long, narrow strips of linen decorated with horizontal bands of embroidery. They were often cut from a loom width of linen, which the selvedge at the top and bottom of the embroidery indicates. The orderly arrangement of patterns on band samplers like this suggests that these embroideries were thoughtfully designed, and seems to support the belief that they were stitched more as learning exercises and demonstrations of technical skill than as design reference works.

By the mid to late 1600s, these samplers were being embroidered by relatively wealthy girls as part of their needlework education. Sampler making constituted the early stages of the curriculum, when the girls were eight or nine years old. The range of stitches found on them can be awesomely extensive; there are ten different, skilfully worked stitched techniques on this one. However, such fine embroidery as this is often thought to be the work of adults – perhaps produced by tutors as model pieces for their pupils to follow. If this is the case here then the reversed letter S in the stitched alphabet is amusing: even teachers are not perfect!

This band sampler also illustrates the use of white and coloured needlelace. Look at the birds worked in coloured silk threads: they have been sewn in detached needlelace stitches, like the gillyflower between them. The pomegranates placed on either side of the flower's stalk are worked in detached stitches over padding. Modest amounts of this padding, which may be sheep's wool, have also been used to fill out the embroidered acorns in the second band from the bottom. The similar bird and plant pattern which is included amongst the whitework bands (here carried out in lacis work) can be traced to a design in Peter Quentel's pattern book *New Kunstlich Boich*, first published in Cologne in 1527.

After stitching a coloured and then a whitework sampler, or demonstrating the techniques in one embroidery as here, the young embroiderer would progress to decorating a variety of objects with different embroidery techniques. Amongst these she may have included a tent-stitched picture, an item in beadwork, and the ultimate virtuoso piece, a casket encrusted with three-dimensional embroidery often called stumpwork or raised work. At this final stage the young embroiderer would be able to make lavish use of the needlelace techniques which she had tackled in her sampler making.

English band sampler worked during the late-seventeenth century by a most accomplished embroiderer

Project 1

FLOWERS WITH STRAWBERRIES

◊

Designed by Muriel Best

This unusual design is based on the seventeenth-century band sampler shown on page 17. It features some of the motifs and stitches used in the original. The flowers and fruit reflect an interest in gardens which has continued to inspire needlewomen over the centuries.

Overlapping bands of pale-pink, mid-pink and pale-green silk noil form the background and the motifs are linked by a meandering line of double running stitch. Some of the flowers and leaves are raised from the surface by padding with felt or thick vilene (pellon) which is then covered with stitching. If it is difficult to obtain coloured silk noil, the natural-coloured noil dyes well.

Although this sampler is not a beginner's piece, it includes a number of stitches and techniques which will appeal to anyone looking for something different to work. It has been designed to give enjoyment while making new discoveries and, besides serving as a reference for future work, it is complete in itself and may also become a family heirloom.

◊

Size (stitched area) 235 x 138mm (9 x 5¼in)
Materials
440 x 340mm (17 x 13¼in) pale-pink silk noil
170 x 340mm (6½ x 13¼in) mid-pink silk noil
145 x 340mm (5½ x 13¼in) pale-green silk noil

Anchor stranded embroidery cotton (floss):
pink 968, 969, 970
green 858, 859, 861
gold 890
fawn 903
DMC flower thread:
pink 2778, 2223, 2329
green 2474, 2732, 2937
fawn 2642
pale fawn 2950
blue 2826, 2828
White felt or thick vilene (pellon) for padding
Crewel needle 10
Tapestry needle 24 or 26 or ballpoint needle

1 Mount pale-pink fabric in a slate or rectangular embroidery frame to keep the work taut and avoid folds and creases.

2 Lay the pale-green band in position at the top and the mid-pink band in position at the bottom of the sampler. The extra fabric allows for the final mounting.

3 Tack (baste) both bands in position. The embroidery stitches will prevent the fabric from fraying.

4 Outline the size of the design with tacking (basting) stitches.

5 Transfer the design (page 20) to the background using the tissue paper method described on page 131.

STITCH GUIDE

Meandering lines: double running stitch using two strands of fawn embroidery cotton (floss).

Leaves on pale-green band: cross stitch using two strands of mid-green and dark-green embroidery cotton (floss).

Carnations: slanting straight stitch using one strand of embroidery cotton (floss), shading petals pale pink to deep pink; calyx mid green.

Rose: detached buttonhole stitch for two petals, using one strand of gold embroidery cotton (floss), and satin stitch for other petals, using two strands of gold embroidery cotton (floss); row at flower

Flowers with Strawberries, by Muriel Best

Tracing guide

20

centre in fawn; fly stitch for centre of rose using deep-pink flower thread; detached buttonhole stitch for leaves using dark-green flower thread.

Buds: satin stitch over a padding of vilene (pellon) – see page 132 – using two strands of mid-green embroidery cotton (floss); work straight stitches on top (see colour illustration) using one strand of dark-green embroidery cotton (floss); one strand of deep pink for the buds and one strand of dark green for the calyx.

Cornflower: detached buttonhole stitch using pale-blue and deep-blue flower threads; bullion knots using three strands of gold embroidery cotton (floss) make the centre; the tips of the petals are decorated with small straight stitches using dark-blue flower thread.

Strawberries: trellis stitch for two strawberries using pale-green, pale-pink and deep-pink flower thread; the third strawberry is worked in detached buttonhole stitch alternating pale-green and deep-pink flower threads; the calyxes are worked in straight stitches with pale-green flower thread. NB The lower strawberry is padded with felt, see page 132.

Leaf: detached buttonhole stitch using dark-green flower thread; the veins are worked in fly stitch using one strand of gold embroidery cotton (floss).

Pomegranate: the centre is worked in bands of satin stitch using two strands of embroidery cotton (floss) in pale pink, mid pink, deep pink and pale green, the middle three bands are padded with vilene (pellon); the rest of the motif is worked in detached buttonhole stitch using pale-fawn flower thread with deep fawn at the centre. Work from the outside into the centre. The leaves are also in detached buttonhole stitch using pale-fawn and pale-blue flower threads.

This detail of the original seventeenth-century sampler shows the fruit and plant pattern which inspired Muriel Best

SONGBIRDS, CARNATIONS AND WHITEWORK

A band sampler with recurring motifs

This band sampler has many similarities with the example on page 17, one of the most striking being the use of the same gillyflower (carnation or pink) motif. Here, the gillyflower appears in the second band above the alphabets, on the other sampler look for it in the first band of coloured embroidery below the stitched alphabet.

It is a fascinating and enjoyable exercise to compare samplers from the same period, to spot similar, or identical designs; and to note not only the different techniques used, but also the varying levels of skill exhibited. The samplers which survive and are widely illustrated do tend to be the most skilled and decorative specimens, but different levels of expertise can be detected among them.

This sampler, which was sewn by someone with the initials H.S., is a very accomplished piece, although K.C., the embroiderer of the sampler on page 17, does seem to have been far more proficient than H.S. in whitework and needlelace techniques and has used them more extensively. H.S. restricted her attempt at cutwork and needlelace fillings to one rather battered and unfinished band of whitework which you can see above her initials and the date 1680. This was still enough to inspire Marion Glover's second sampler entitled *Whitework* (see page 30).

In fact, this panel of the original sampler is the reverse of the work: H.S. seems to have sewn different patterns from each side of the cloth. The remainder of her sampler is worked predominantly in cross and linear stitches such as running stitch and double running stitch, which have given her patterns a sketchy appearance. K.C. filled in her patterns with a denser covering of stitches using a wider variety of thread colours than H.S., who was happy to restrict her coloured work to three pale colours: salmon pink, blue and green. The colours hardly vary between the right and wrong side of the work, so presumably they have changed little in over three hundred years. Both these samplers carry complete (accepting some omissions as deliberate) and incomplete stitched alphabets worked in coloured silks and white linen in three different techniques: cross stitch, satin stitch and eyelet stitch.

Many people have pondered on the appearance of the stitched alphabets, inscriptions and verse on late seventeenth-century band samplers. Some have seen a link between the embroidered alphabets and the trend developing in affluent homes at that time of marking household linen with family initials and numbers for identification purposes. Before the advent of indelible inks, stitchery would have been a practical long-term method of marking linen. The stitched verse and inscriptions which were increasingly included in samplers during the later decades of the 1600s may be an indication that the wealthy young girls who worked them were literate. However, different levels of literacy are reflected in the stitchery: omissions, misformed letters and words run together (in sampler verse) suggest that many young embroiderers had not fully mastered their letters when they worked their embroideries; and

English band sampler dated 1680

This detail of the 1680 band sampler shows the naked boxer figures. They might once have represented lovers

perhaps saw the alphabet simply as a sequence of shapes with as yet little or no meaning for them. The omission of the letters J and U from these embroidered alphabets was not a mistake by the embroiderer: during the seventeenth century the letters I and V were used for J and U and frequently the letter Q was worked as a reversed P. Look at the various attempts at the alphabet in this sampler and the one on page 17: neither embroiderer has included the letters J or U, and both have stitched reverse Ps to represent Q.

Although stylised flower and plant patterns dominate seventeenth-century band samplers, bird and animal motifs were popular too. Typically flower and plant motifs were stitched as repeating wave patterns which had their origins in sixteenth- and early seventeenth-century

embroidery designs. Often very similar or even the same motifs and patterns can be found on samplers which were stitched miles and years apart, suggesting the use of a widely available common design source. Some sampler motifs (as with the birds shown here) have been identified as coming from printed embroidery pattern books, but many are thought to have been copied from other samplers. This latter practice has lead to some stitched motifs evolving into mutant forms of a printed original.

Figure motifs appear occasionally in samplers of this period. Sometimes they are anonymous seventeenth-century people, but more often they are representations of Biblical characters. Amongst the Embroiderers' Guild's seventeenth-century samplers there are several which include versions of the figure motif

Here, the carnation or gillyflower patterns on the 1680 hand sampler are shown in greater detail

known as the boxer. Three boxers were stitched by H.S. on to this sampler. Here they are depicted naked, which was common, but occasionally you will see them clothed, as on the Contents pages of this book. Whether clothed or naked the boxer assumes the same sideways stance with one arm upraised. He derives his modern name from this pugilistic attitude. However, the object he invariably clutches, and which is sometimes called a trophy, would most certainly hinder a bout of fisticuffs. Historians have speculated on the origin of this little figure, but it is now believed that he could have evolved from images in sixteenth-century pattern books of a young man presenting a gift to his lover. Through time and the habit of using older embroideries to copy from, the young man's amorous ad-

vances have become mistaken for aggressive behaviour. He also lost his clothes and his lover. She seems to have become the large stylised flower which is often placed between rows of boxers; you can see this on H.S.'s sampler.

By looking closely at the gillyflower and bird pattern on page 17 it is possible to detect two inverted birds worked in satin stitch and double running stitches and detached needlelace. Now look carefully at H.S.'s sampler: the third pattern band below the boxers carries the same or a very similar little bird. He is easily missed here partly because of his small scale, but also because he has been outlined in simple running stitches in contrast to the richer treatment given on the first sampler. This is the little bird which Marion Glover has featured in the following sampler *Songbirds and Carnations.*

SONGBIRDS AND CARNATIONS

◊

Designed by Marion Glover

From a wealth of motifs on the seven-teenth-century band sampler on page 23, formal carnations and birds have been chosen for this delightful design. The carnation, or gillyflower, grew in many gardens of the time and is frequently seen in embroidery.

The sampler is worked mainly in cross stitch with some double running stitches. The varied spacing of the cross stitches gives different effects, and the sampler is further enlivened by the use of metallic gold thread on the birds. Because of its simplicity, this sampler will have a wide appeal.

The carnation at the centre of the design could also be worked on its own to make a delightful pincushion or other small gift. The border could easily be adapted for use on bed or table linen. Other colours could be substituted for the background or the embroidery threads.

◊

Size (stitched area) 220 x 220mm (8½ x 8½in)
Materials
390 x 390mm (15 x 15in) ivory 14-count Aida
DMC stranded embroidery cotton (floss):
turquoise 598, 828
pink 3354, 353, 948
Elizabeth Stuart gold cord shade 1, or Madeira Metallic Effect Yarn shade 3003
Tapestry needle 14 or 16

1 This sampler may be worked in the hand or in a frame. Before starting to stitch, study the chart (page 28) carefully to be sure of the spacing. It may be helpful to tack (baste) threads across the fabric and down the fabric so that they cross at the exact centre. With the exception of the bird motifs, the sampler is worked in cross stitch throughout. Keep the tension of the stitches as even as possible and make sure that the top strokes of the stitches all lie in the same direction.

2 Following the chart, begin to stitch at the centre with turquoise 598. This gives a point of reference for the rest of the work.

3 Outline the centre carnation motifs with pink 3354. Fill in with pinks 353 and 948, using the colour illustration as a guide.

4 With turquoise 828 begin the inner row of the stepped grid, checking the position against the centre flowers. When you are satisfied, complete the two outer rows.

5 The four corner grid motifs and the four centre grid motifs are worked next, following the chart and the colour illustration.

6 With turquoise 598 work the outlines of the border, carefully checking the placing of the stitches. Work the small rectangles with pink 3354. Complete the border by filling in with pink 353.

7 Work the birds with metallic gold thread in double running stitch. Each bird has a single gold cross-stitch eye.

8 Using three strands of the Madeira thread, or the gold cord, work the stamens of the central carnations in cross stitch.

Songbirds and Carnations, by Marion Glover

	DMC
	828
	598
	948
	3354
	948
	CORD SHADE 1

Songbirds and Carnations chart

Whitework chart

Project 3

WHITEWORK

◊

Designed by Marion Glover

◊

White embroidery on a white background has its own charm, with the added advantage that it will be at home in any setting. Early embroiderers would progress to whitework after satisfactorily completing a band sampler in coloured threads. Some of the most popular stitches used in the complex and detailed whitework samplers of the seventeenth century have been simplified to make this sampler fairly easy to work. The contrasting textures of satin stitch, chain stitch and French knots, worked with a slightly shiny thread, are seen to advantage against the self-coloured background.

The design could also be used for a small sampler cushion, perhaps filled with pot-pourri or herbs. The motif in the centre could be used separately, and the border is equally versatile. Both the motif and the border could be repeated, re-arranged or extended if required.

◊

Size (stitched area) 165 x 165mm (6¼ x 6¼in)
Materials
360 x 360mm (14 x 14in) 26-count cotton, linen or cotton-and linen-mixture fabric
360 x 360mm (14 x 14in) piece of firmly woven cotton fabric to back the top fabric
1 ball of white DMC pearl cotton No 8. (Three strands of white stranded embroidery cotton (floss) may be used as an alternative)
Crewel needle 14 or 16 (10 or 12 if stranded cotton is used)

1 Trace the design (page 29) with an embroidery transfer pencil (see page 131), and iron on to top fabric.

2 Place the top fabric and backing fabric together, making sure that the grains match, and tack (baste) together. Mount in a 310mm (12in) circular frame or in a rectangular (slate) frame.

3 With the fabric held at medium tension, and using the chart as a guide, work the chain stitch lines.

4 Now tighten the tension of the fabric and work the satin-stitch areas. The stitches should lie closely together and evenly, with a neat edge.

5 Complete the stitching with the French knots.

6 If the sampler becomes a little grubby while working, or if any of the transfer outlines remain visible, it may be washed gently by hand. Rinse well and, when nearly dry, lay face down on a thick towel and iron carefully.

Detail of Marion Glover's design

Whitework, by Marion Glover

COMMEMORATIVE HEARTS

Eighteenth-century inscriptions

This interesting sampler was designed in the old way of seventeenth-century band samplers even though it was worked in the 1700s. Although it is quite long at 35.7cm (14in) it was originally longer, but at some time during its life the embroidery was chopped up. No one knows why or when this was, or what happened to the rest of the sampler which is frustrating and sad, partly because of the loss of the lovely embroidery, but also because any information it may have contained about the embroiderer and her sampler has also been lost.

Nevertheless, what remains is certainly very pleasing. Silk threads have been used to embroider alphabets, motifs and patterns, and two inscriptions in bands across the linen in a variety of stitches which include the following: Algerian eye, satin, tent, cross and marking cross stitches, Florentine and back stitches. The centrally positioned band of motifs is particularly appealing. It includes serrated leaf motifs which may be interpretations of the prickly holly leaf, which is a type of foliage design rarely encountered on historic needlework. Richard Shorleyker's embroidery pattern book *A Schole-house for the Needle*, published in London in 1624, did include motifs of a holly leaf, and a holly leaf with berry spray, but these do not seem to have enjoyed the wide appeal of other motifs and patterns. The second plant motif embroidered within this sampler band shows leaf and berry sprays which look very much like mistletoe sprigs; again this plant is a rarity in historic embroidery design.

Heart-shaped motifs also feature in this band. They became popular with sampler makers during the eighteenth century, although what they meant to early embroiderers is not known. Today they have either sentimental or religious connotations, but they could have been used on this sampler for purely decorative purposes, as may also have been the case with the crown and coronet motifs.

Crowns and coronets began to appear on samplers during the later seventeenth century, and are generally regarded as marking devices which were used on household furnishings and costume to identify the titled owner and his status. They made regular appearances on samplers throughout the eighteenth century, and can frequently be found on nineteenth-century marking samplers. How many of these sampler makers were part of a titled family or were in the service of such? Surely far more embroiderers stitched these motifs than ever had the need or opportunity to use them for identification purposes.

The band of diamond shapes worked in Florentine stitch reminds us of the increased use of canvas-work embroidery during the early eighteenth century. From the later 1600s onwards changes in furniture design tended to promote the use of embroidered canvas as a decorative and durable upholstery material. Padded and winged chairs, single seats, or sets of dining chairs provided scope for the professional or domestic embroiderer to display their skills. Floral designs reminiscent of still life paintings, sequences of narrative scenes and geometric patterns were all embroidered in canvas-work techniques.

The Florentine stitch on this sampler allowed multi-coloured geometric designs to be worked in silk or woollen yarns. The skilful shading and the zigzag patterns used probably gave such work one of its alternative titles: flame stitch.

The dyes, once vibrant as the reverse of the sampler shows, have faded to pastel shades which although they are attractive do make deciphering the stitched inscriptions difficult. However, perseverance reveals the wording to be as follows:

The Loss of time is much the loss of grace is more the loss of Christ is such as no man can restore

Remember man as you past by as you are now so once was I as I am now so must you be prepare yourself to follow me

The embroiderer gave no thought to line length or punctuation.

Early British eighteenth-century sampler which uses the band-pattern format

Project 4

COMMEMORATIVE

◊

Designed by Lesley Barnett

Anniversaries call for something special. This golden wedding sampler, inspired by the two hearts on the eighteenth-century sampler on page 33, would be the perfect present on such an occasion. The quotation is from the *Song of Songs*.

The initials and dates on the sampler can easily be adapted for other anniversaries or special occasions, as the sampler includes two complete alphabets and a set of figures. Similarly, the colour of the background and threads could be changed as appropriate, or a little gold or silver thread could be added. A wedding sampler might be stitched on the same fabric as that used for the bride's dress.

This sampler is worked by laying a counted fabric on top of the silk background and stitching through both, which keeps the stitches even. When the work is finished the threads of the top fabric are withdrawn, leaving the stitches on the silk background. This may seem complicated but, providing a loosely woven top fabric is used, it is not difficult to do. Alternatively, the chart can be used to work on canvas or counted fabric. Simple stitches are used throughout.

◊

Size (stitched area) 385 x 245mm (15 x 9½in)
Materials
600 x 450mm (24 x 18in) pale-yellow silk dupion
600 x 450mm (24 x 18in) fine cotton fabric (not too densely woven) for backing
450 x 300mm (18 x 12in) 27-count fabric, eg Jobelan
Madeira stranded silk:
blue 1003, 1005, 1105, 1107, 1711 (one skein of each)
green 1114, 1212, 1214, 1312 (one skein of each)
green 1407 (two skeins)
cream 2014 (two skeins)
gold 2209, 2211, 2213 (one skein of each); 2208, 2210 (two skeins of each)
Tapestry needle 26

1 Mount the cotton backing fabric in a rectangular (slate) frame. Lay the silk fabric on top of the backing and the counted fabric on top of the silk. Make sure that the grain of all three fabrics is matched exactly.

2 Tack (baste) the three fabrics together, starting in the centre and working outwards vertically and horizontally at 50mm (2in) intervals. Keep the fabrics flat and straight. Tacking (basting) stitches can be removed as the work progresses.

3 Use two strands of stranded silk or embroidery cotton (floss) throughout. For the background of the quotation, and the alphabet below it, use two tones of gold in the needle, or a variegated thread, to add subtlety. Make stitches with two movements, up and down, keeping the needle vertical. Avoid splitting the threads of the counted fabric.

4 On the chart: one square represents one cross stitch (one block); two satin stitches side by side are worked either vertically or horizontally, forming one block. See chart for length of the stitches.

5 Begin stitching with the two cross-stitch hearts just above the centre of the sampler. Then add the dates in double running stitch and the initials in eyelets using the cross stitch alphabet as a guide (each cross represents an eyelet worked over four threads). Work out from this area, one band at a time, starting each row of stitches in the centre and working outwards. The diamond pattern enclosing the initials may need adjusting to accommodate other letters.

6 When the embroidery is finished, remove the counted fabric thread by thread, starting with the vertical threads one at a time from each side. Lift the threads with a tapestry needle. If any of the embroidery stitches are a little loose, adjust by pulling gently at the back.

7 Stretch the embroidery (see page 132) before mounting and framing.

Commemorative, by Lesley Barnett

COMMEMORATIVE

DOUBLE
RUNNING
STITCH AND
SATIN STITCH

SATIN STITCH

EYELET STITCH

CROSS STITCH
LETTERS

CROSS STITCH

EYELET STITCH

CROSS STITCH
LETTERS

SATIN STITCH

SATIN STITCH

VERTICAL
SATIN STITCH

HORIZONTAL
SATIN STITCH

EYELET STITCH
TRIANGLES
AND INITIALS

DOUBLE
RUNNING
STITCH
OUTLINE
AND DATE

CROSS STITCH
HEARTS

CENTRE

RUNNING
STITCH

SATIN STITCH
(MIX COLOURS)

DOUBLE
RUNNING
STITCH

HERRINGBONE
STITCH

CROSS STITCH

SHADED SATIN
STITCH

EYELET STITCH
AND DIAGONAL
SATIN STITCH

CROSS STITCH

HERRINGBONE
STITCH

DIAGONAL
SATIN STITCH

DOUBLE
RUNNING
STITCH

SATIN STITCH
BLOCKS

DOUBLE
RUNNING
STITCH

SATIN STITCH

WORKER'S
INITIALS

MADEIRA

| 1003 | 1105 | 1711 | 1212 | 1312 | 2014 | 2209 | 2211 |
| 1005 | 1107 | 1114 | 1214 | 1407 | 2208 | 2210 | 2213 |

37

COUNTED TRANQUILLITY

A whitework sampler – subtle and refined

This delicate whitework sampler has an unusual layout. The rectangle of very fine cotton has been divided into four columns, three of which have been embroidered with horizontal band patterns in the conventional way. The signature and date ML 1733 embroidered beneath the third column implies that this is the end: perhaps the embroiderer ran out of sufficient enthusiasm, or patterns, to work the final strip. The patterns themselves date back to those found in sixteenth- and seventeenth-century embroidery pattern books. Here they are executed with a subtlety and refinement quite in keeping with the elegance which became a feature of much eighteenth-century embroidery as the decades passed by.

This sampler has the look of one which functioned in the old way, that is as a record of patterns and stitches, and perhaps it was used as such. Whitework embroidery was frequently used to decorate eighteenth-century costume pieces. Although coiling plant motifs and patterns of large, almost abstract or stylised flower heads were popular during the early part of the century, this sampler's linear patterns were frequently used as fillings within the larger shapes. The play of light on the stitches would create contrasts of pattern and texture which looked most effective on eighteenth-century whitework waistcoats and delicate Dresden-work aprons, fichus and sleeve ruffles.

British whitework sampler, signed and dated M.L. 1733

Project 5

COUNTED PATTERNS

◊

Designed by Jenny Bullen

◊

The eighteenth-century sampler (see page 38-39) which inspired this modern one was worked in repeating patterns with fine white thread on a fine white fabric. Its air of tranquillity is preserved in the contemporary version. Bands of patterns in counted satin stitch are divided by lines of four-sided stitch pulled tightly.

This sampler is ideal for beginners as counted satin stitch and four-sided stitch are not difficult to work and no other stitches are used.

The sampler looks attractive stitched in white on a pastel background as shown here. The way the light falls on the satin stitches shows up the patterns, and the sheen of the thread contrasts with the texture made by the four-sided stitch. A natural-coloured background could be used as an alternative, or brightly coloured threads on a white fabric. You might like to match the colours to the colour scheme of the room in which the embroidery is to be placed.

◊

Size (stitched area) 230 x 190mm (9 x 7¼in)
Materials
500 x 380mm (19¾ x 15in) 28-count Jobelan (blue was used for this sampler)
1 skein DMC stranded embroidery cotton (floss) to match the background colour of your choice
1 ball DMC pearl cotton No 8 Blanc Neige
Tapestry needle 22 or 24

1 Neaten the edges of the fabric with overcasting or machine zigzag stitch before starting work.

2 Crease the fabric lightly to find the centre and mark the horizontal and vertical lines made with tacking (basting) stitches.

3 The embroidery can be worked in a frame but it may be easier to work the four-sided stitch in the hand.

4 Begin working from the centre using the chart (page 43) as a guide. Using pearl cotton, start with a pattern of satin stitches. Then work a row of four-sided stitch with two strands of embroidery cotton (floss) in the needle.

5 Continue in this way until all the horizontal rows of embroidery have been worked. Complete the sampler with the frame of four-sided stitch.

6 When the embroidery is finished it may need stretching if the pulled thread stitches have distorted it at all. See page 132 for stretching and mounting instructions.

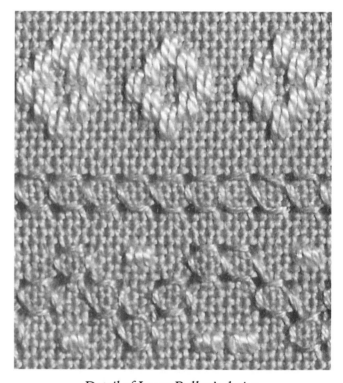

Detail of Jenny Bullen's design

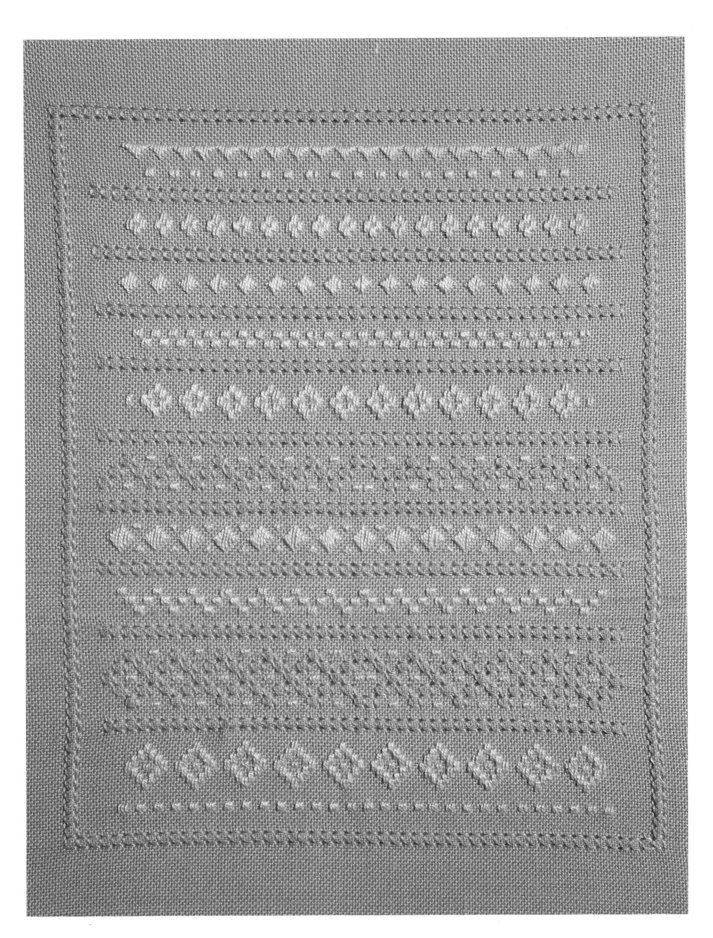

Counted patterns, by Jenny Bullen

Detail of the eighteenth-century whitework sampler

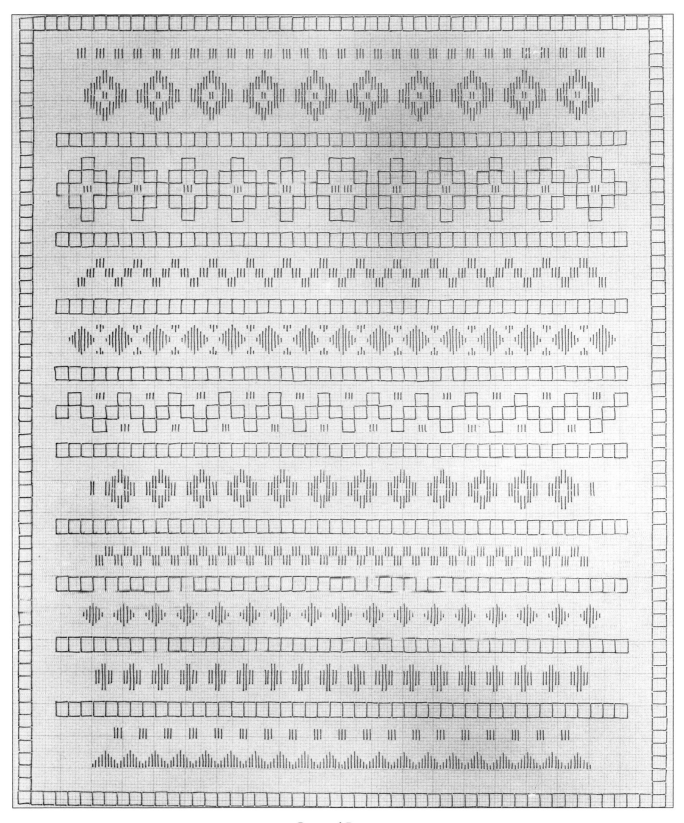

Counted Patterns

HOUSES AND CROSS STITCH

A 'traditional' sampler – the shape of things to come

It was during the eighteenth century that the type of embroidery now regarded as the traditional sampler took shape. The sampler shown opposite is just such an embroidery, one which many people think of as a typical sampler: that is, a square or rectangular panel with a central motif or stitched verse, framed by an embroidered border of plant or flower patterns. As the eighteenth century advanced a taste for enclosing the body of the sampler design within an embroidered border became popular. This reflected a growing fashion for exhibiting samplers so that everyone could see, and hopefully admire, the level of skill achieved.

Houses and buildings maintained an abiding popularity with sampler designers. We often find ourselves speculating on whether the buildings were real or imaginary, and because we like to see samplers as records of a person's life we willingly believe that the motifs embroidered upon them probably held some personal significance for the embroiderer. Some of the embroidered buildings which appear on samplers are thought to represent the schools and orphanages in which the embroiderers were taught or lived. However, it would be unwise to assume that every fine house stitched was an illustration of the embroiderer's home.

The house embroidered on this sampler is certainly a very fine brick-built building. With its double-fronted aspect, columns and portico, it is more a mansion than a house. Similar examples can be found on other samplers. Were these actual houses or dream homes representing eighteenth-century aspirations?

Because of its central position we do tend to focus on this elegant house but it would be a pity to miss the other interesting features on this sampler. One of the most obvious is the inclusion of names stitched on either side of the house: S. Ewart, I. Ewart; Mary Sawers, E. Sawers. Who were these people? Perhaps they were grandparents of the embroiderer, and the rather cramped M.S. stitched above the broad red door were her own initials. This sampler is thought to be a late eighteenth-century embroidery and in its layout contrasts markedly with the long narrow band samplers of the seventeenth century; but it has not entirely lost sight of its ancestor. Look at the wave pattern which borders the sampler, and more particularly the two highly stylised band patterns stitched across the top part. These are so similar to the band patterns which were a feature of the seventeenth-century samplers and are clearly the origin of these later patterns. It is interesting to see how long-lived some motifs and patterns can be, even becoming, as the wave border does, a traditional part of sampler design.

This sampler is a most accomplished piece. The embroiderer has used five stitches to work her sampler: rococo, tent, cross, rice and back stitches. The design is beautifully planned and drawn; and is embroidered with considerable prowess revealing a talented hand at work. We can only speculate on who this embroiderer was, whether a young girl at the end of her childhood 'training', or a tutor demonstrating her skills to a pupil or a future employer. A glance will show that this sampler has been nibbled by moths, making holes in the woollen ground fabric. Towards the end of the eighteenth century a considerable number of samplers used wool rather than linen as their basis, and consequently most of them have been attacked by moth.

Pictorial sampler embroidered in Britain during the late-eighteenth century

Project 6

HOUSE AND GARDEN

◊

Designed by Jane Greenoff

Based on the eighteenth-century pictorial sampler on page 45, the restrained colour and harmonious design of this contemporary version will appeal to many embroiderers. It perfectly recaptures the spirit of the past but, when framed, would look charming in any modern setting.

The sampler is worked mainly in cross stitch, with the addition of some French knots, Algerian eye stitch, back stitch and queen (rococo) stitch. If preferred, cross stitches or tiny beads can be substituted for the French knots. The sampler is well within the capacity of most embroiderers, with the possible exception of complete beginners, and will be a pleasure to stitch.

◊

Size (stitched area) 360 x 255mm (14 x 10in)

Materials

565 x 465mm (22 x 18in) ivory 28-count pure linen or 14-count ivory Aida

DMC stranded embroidery cotton (floss):
off-white 712
honey 437
dark plum 3685
lime green 471
dark grey 317
red 304
dark blue 930
dark pink 3350
sage green 320
medium brown 611
old gold 729
salmon pink 352
coffee 436
dark stone 640
pale honey 738
stone 3032
dark green 936
olive green 470
lichen green 733

Tapestry needle 24 or 26

STITCH GUIDE

The sampler is stitched in cross stitch worked over two threads of the linen in each direction (or one block of Aida) unless stated otherwise on the chart. Additional stitch instructions are also given on the chart. Most of the design is worked with two strands of embroidery cotton (floss) in the needle.

French knots are stitched with two strands of embroidery cotton (floss) and two winds over the needle, except for the birds' eyes. These are worked with one strand only.

The *back stitch* outline of the house is worked with one strand of stone 3032.

The *green outline pattern* at the top of the design is worked in back stitch with two strands of lime green 471.

Algerian eye stitch is worked over four threads of the linen using two strands of olive green 470. To work the *four large strawberries*, outline the shape in one strand of red 304. Fill the space with queen stitch, using one strand of dark pink or red chosen at random, and working from the top down.

1 Hem the raw edges of the fabric to prevent fraying.

2 Fold the fabric in four, press lightly and mark the central lines with tacking (basting) stitches. These will be removed when the design is completed.

3 Working from the chart, start in the centre and stitch outwards.

House and Garden, by Jane Greenoff

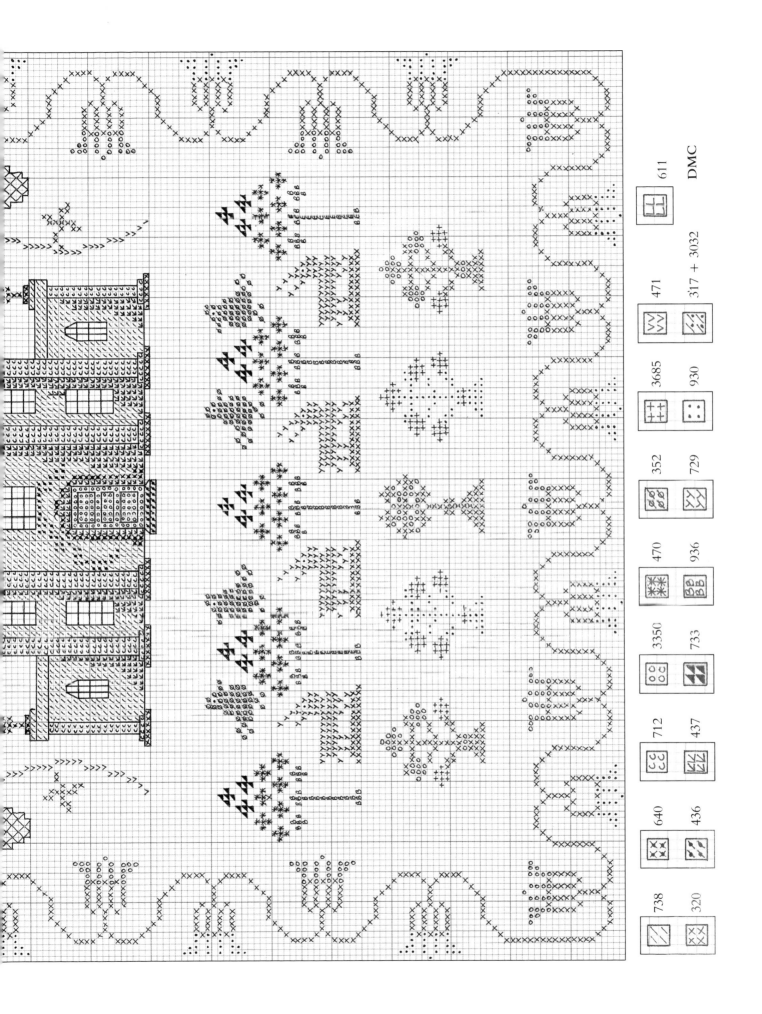

DMC

611

471 | 317 + 3032

3685 | 930

352 | 729

470 | 936

3350 | 733

712 | 437

640 | 436

738 | 320

RURAL LIFE AND A FAMILY TREE

Stitched building motifs – an individual touch

This charming sampler was embroidered in 1784. It is unusual in that it illustrates such a variety of stitched building motifs. These are a cottage, a church, a tall double-fronted building which may be the manor house or a school, and a multi-coloured palace perched on top of a very steep hill.

Apart from the palace, which is reminiscent of palace motifs in Stuart embroideries, it is tempting to believe that these buildings were known to the embroiderer. Perhaps she passed them every day as she took her 'constitutional' through the village, or gazed at them through the parlour window? Certainly this sampler has a more markedly individual feel to it than many other samplers: look at the handsome carriage beneath the three-storey building on pages 52-53. A little female head peeps out from above the carriage door which carries the letters A.R. (is this a self-portrait of the embroiderer Ann Richmond?) whilst a much more rustic cart pulled by three black horses is appropriately sited by the country cottage.

The large trees which stand on either side of the three-storey building are distinctive. If a tree motif is found on seventeenth-century samplers it is usually a version of a fruit tree, and is often said to represent the Tree of Knowledge in the Garden of Eden. During the eighteenth century a wider variety of trees was embroidered upon samplers. A range of stylised pyramid and diamond-shaped tree motifs were popular, perhaps reflecting an eighteenth-century vogue for topiary and formal gardens.

Weeping willows feature in many later eighteenth-century samplers and pictorial embroideries. The willow has associations with loss and mourning and consequently was often used as a motif in mourning samplers or pictorial pieces with an overriding sentimental tone.

The two leafy trees which Ann Richmond stitched are quite unusual, and may be intended as sycamore or maple trees with their stylised trefoil-shaped leaves. The appearance of the maple-leaf motif in samplers is often held as evidence that the embroidery is American, originating in the New England area. Indeed the sawtooth border on Ann Richmond's sampler is also sometimes regarded as an American sampler design trait. This might explain why Ann Richmond's sampler is so different from other samplers thought to be British: but there is evidence for and against it being an American embroidery. Look at the church, it is so English: but perhaps this motif was copied from an earlier embroidery, pattern or illustration brought over from Britain to the United States. Frustratingly, the origins of this sampler must remain a mystery for now. More research is required before we can say with confidence from which side of the Atlantic it came.

Detail of Ann Richmond's sampler

50

This charming sampler was worked by Ann Richmond in 1784; it is possibly British or American

Project 7

FAMILY TREE

◊

Designed by Mary Jenkins

Inspired by the eighteenth-century sampler showing scenes from rural life (see pages 52–53), this sampler records details of life in the modern world, with a house and garden, and family pets. The quotation is taken from Padraic Colum's poem *An Old Woman of the Roads*.

The design could be adapted to fit most families by changing some details. It could even include the postcode! The large tree on the right could bear the names of members of the family, their relatives and friends, making it a real 'family' tree. A sampler like this would make a most appropriate housewarming present or a gift to mark the arrival of a new baby.

This sampler as it stands is not appropriate for beginners because it uses a variety of canvas-work stitches. However, beginners could stitch entirely or partly in cross stitch or tent stitch over one intersection of canvas.

◊

Size (stitched area) 270 x 205mm (10½ x 7⅞in)

Materials

430 x 360mm (16¾ x 14in) off-white 22-count canvas
1 skein each of the following DMC stranded
embroidery cotton (floss):
grey 3022
silver 927
turquoise 924
dark green 606
jade green 991
blue 792
dark gold 831
light gold 832
light green 3347
light olive 581
dark olive 580
very dark grey 844
brown 610
dark brick 355
light brick 356
pink 950
variegated yellow 104
variegated red 57
variegated green 94
variegated pale blue 67
black
white
Tapestry needle 24

Use five strands of embroidery cotton (floss) for the vertical stitches, three strands for the diagonal stitches, two strands for the cross and rococo stitches, and one strand for the back stitch.

To work the textured stitches, outline the shape in tent stitch with one strand of thread, then fill and cover this outline with the appropriate stitch.

Use the variegated threads for the sky, the geraniums, parts of the flower border, the leaves of the tree, and other flowers and plants.

1 Tack (baste) threads down the exact centre of the canvas, and at the exact centre across, to act as guidelines.

2 Begin at the centre point by working the branches of the tree, and then the trunk. Do not add the leaves yet.

3 Work the gate and the wall, counting the threads from the centre point.

4 Start the border on both sides from the centre outwards. Work the outline of the inside border first; then fill in, but leave the base.

5 The 'bare bones' are now worked and everything else can be counted from them. Work from the top down. Finally work the base of the border.

STITCH GUIDE

Anything not listed is worked in tent stitch.

Gate: tent, slanting Gobelin and back stitches with a long diagonal stitch overlaid.
Wall: elongated cushion stitch.
Top of wall: satin-stitch triangle.

Family Tree, by Mary Jenkins

Border: tent, cross, satin and slanting Gobelin stitches.

Thatch: satin and split-Gobelin stitches.

Chimney: brick stitch over two threads.

Windows: tent and slanting Gobelin stitches overlaid with long threads.

Door: tent and slanting Gobelin stitches.

Porch roof: satin stitch.

Porch sides: tent stitch overworked in cross stitch.

Garden: tent, slanting Gobelin and satin stitches with French knots.

Topiary: French knots mixing two greens.

Trees: (from left to right): rococo, cross and brick stitches over 4 threads.

Hedge by the trees: diagonal mosaic stitch.

Railings: long threads laid over tent-stitch background.

Beehive: slanting Gobelin stitch.

Bees: French knots.

Path: tent stitch overlaid with random cross stitches.

Poodle: French knots.

Hedge: velvet stitch worked upside down.

Verse: back stitch.

Date and surrounding border: cross stitch.

Leaves on tree: leaf and diagonal leaf stitches.

Animals: cross stitch outlined with back stitch.

Eyes of cat and squirrel: French knots.

Flowerpot: tent and back stitches with eyelets.

FAMILY TREE

A little house, a house of my own
Out of the wind and the rain's way

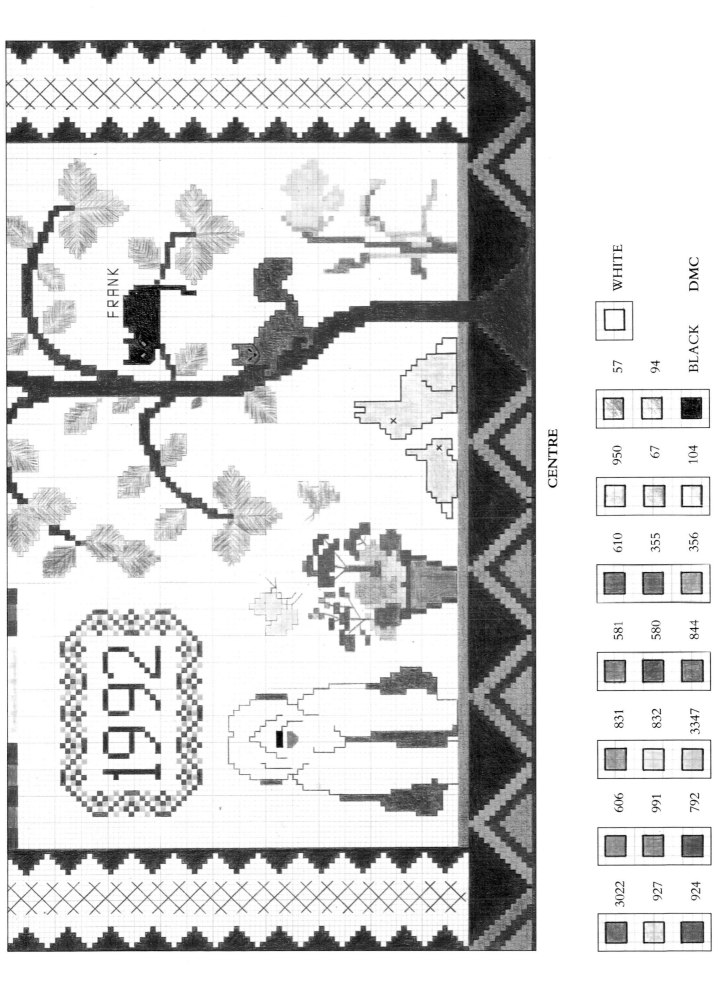

CENTRE

3022	927	924
606	991	792
831	832	3347
581	580	844
610	355	356
950	67	104
57	94	BLACK
WHITE		DMC

FRANK

1992

A Utilitarian Work of Art

Darning sampler – decorative and practical

Towards the end of the eighteenth century darning samplers made their appearance in Britain and grew in popularity amongst sampler makers. Surviving examples are usually dated between c1770 and 1820, although darning samplers continued to be made for many years after this, even into the twentieth century. However, the finest and most ornamental darning samplers are usually those embroidered during the later 1700s and early 1800s. Dutch, Danish and German darning samplers made much earlier in the eighteenth century are often offered as evidence that the vogue for this type of embroidery travelled from those countries.

The darning sampler shown here is a very decorative specimen, and was probably embroidered during the late 1700s. The ground fabric is a loosely woven, coarse linen canvas which has been decorated with a variety of darned (and pulled fabric work) patterns using a range of coloured silk threads. Some of the 'darns' are woven in and out of the warp and weft threads of the ground linen to imitate the patterns of different fabric weaves. Other patches are more ambitious in that they are attached to the ground fabric around their edges only, and do, in fact, create a secondary layer of interwoven threads which lie above the ground fabric and are virtually independent of it. Rightly proud of her work, the embroiderer has added her initials T.A. It is sad for us that she did not provide further information by adding the date of her embroidery, as many of her contemporaries did.

Darning is a functional technique, and one which was of particular value before our own age of cheap mass-produced fabrics which often use synthetic fibres and are therefore durable. In earlier centuries the ability to repair worn fabrics would have been a valuable and also very necessary skill; and judging by the highly ornamental content of many early darning samplers it was a skill which embroiderers were determined to exhibit with pride and panache.

American Quaker schoolmistresses gave their pupils instruction in stitching darning samplers, and their work was reputedly modelled on the utilitarian form of needlework produced in Britain at the Ackworth School in Yorkshire. Certainly the American Quaker darning samplers were not elaborate and ornamental at all, and were evidently produced in order to teach girls a practical skill rather than a fancy accomplishment. These down-to-earth darning samplers have more in common with the functional darning samplers stitched in British boarding schools and orphanages during the nineteenth century than the earlier highly decorative pieces such as the sampler illustrated here.

Contemporary designer Jennie Parry has used the corner blocks composed of four cubes and the four large crosses as the basis of her modern darning sampler, which is illustrated on page 61.

This very decorative darning sampler was probably stitched in Britain during the late-eighteenth century

DARNING SAMPLER

Designed by Jennie Parry

The delicate stitchery on the eighteenth-century darning sampler (page 59) transforms a utilitarian form of needlework into a work of art. This decorative aspect of the darning stitch has been used here to make an exciting modern sampler. Colour, pattern and direction of stitch combine to make a geometric design which changes according to the angle from which it is viewed – some parts of the sampler appear to be three-dimensional. Rather than hang it on a wall, you may prefer to display this sampler under the glass top of a coffee table or tray. If you decide to frame the sampler, it can be mounted square or diamond-wise and finished with a fringe, as illustrated, or a hem.

The darning stitch looks complicated but is fairly easy. The surface darning stitch is more difficult, but you can leave out these areas altogether if you wish. Experienced embroiderers will find the surface darning challenging but fascinating to do.

Size (including fringe) 360 x 360mm (14 x 14in)
Materials
500 x 500mm (19 x 19in) 20-count natural linen scrim
1 skein each of the following DMC coton à broder:
yellow 444
lime green 907
green 700
jade 943
blue 796
purple 552
red 666
orange 947
Tacking (basting) cotton
2 Tapestry needles 24

Work on a piece of scrim 500 x 500mm (19 x 19in). On a spare piece of fabric practise blocks of darning stitch, eg over two threads, under two threads, moving on one thread each row to make the twill effect; or over three threads, under one, over one, under one, etc. There is no need to use a frame, just pick up several groups of threads at a time.

Start from the centre of an area wherever possible, leaving enough thread as a 'tail' to complete the row in the opposite direction. Stitch to the end of the first row, turn, and work back to the centre. Using a second needle, thread the tail and work the rest of the first row. Darn the end back into the pattern to finish, taking care that stitches do not show on the surface. Then continue with the first needle.

If you have to unpick, take care not to distort previous stitching. It may be better to darn back rather than unthread the needle and withdraw the thread.

Surface darning in two colours:
A thread in one colour is darned in the usual way, then brought to the surface and left as a long horizontal stitch before darning to the end of the row. Allow two empty threads for turning.

The second colour is darned vertically through the fabric. Where it meets the long stitches it weaves through them (under two threads, over two threads) before darning to the end as shown on the chart. See also diagrams on page 138.

1 Fold fabric in half in both directions to establish the centre. Tack (baste) along the crease lines, vertically and horizontally, counting carefully and using running stitch over two threads, under two threads.

2 Repeat, tacking (basting) from the centre outwards diagonally to each corner.

3 With *blue* thread, work *centre star*, beginning at the centre hole, with the pattern (over three, under one) four times for eight rows. The negative version (under three, over one) is worked for seven rows. You may find it easier to work this from the back, and then catch or link into the turning threads of the previous section to turn for the next row. Refer to the colour illustration and use the chart as a guide to colour, the length of the stitches and the number of rows to be worked.

Darning Sampler, by Jennie Parry

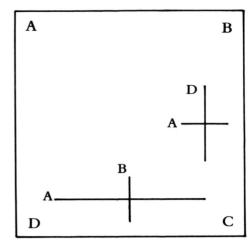

Choice of colours for surface darning

Detail of the central motif on the original sampler

4 Count 40 threads out from the *centre* and establish *red row*, working from the centre tacking line.

5 Work the opposite side in the same way. Take care that the slope of the twill is in the same direction.

6 *Green band:* Count 40 threads from the centre. Follow the line to the corner with the red row. Leave a long tail of thread and stitch, sharing the red holes as shown on the chart. Complete the first row to the other side using a second needle.

7 Begin *zigzag area* with *lime green* (middle row). Work one row of *yellow* and one row of *jade* on either side, the needle going under one thread and over one thread.

8 Count 35 threads from *red* and *green* bands to establish and tack (baste) out the ribbon border rows, and a further 20 threads for the edge of the work. Each corner is 40-threads square, and composed of four squares, each 20 threads by 20 threads.

9 *Ribbon border:* Begin in the centre of each side with one row of *red*, three rows of *purple* and two rows of *blue*.

10 Each *corner* includes two empty threads for turning in each section. The blocks are rotated to reflect the light and pattern (see diagram *right*).

11 *Edging:* Count ten threads out from the ribbon border and start from the centre of each side. Using

red thread, work back stitches over four threads, pulling each stitch tightly before going on to the next.

12 *Finishing:* Remove all tacking (basting) threads. Press from the back of the work. Count 30 threads from the line of red back stitches on each side and withdraw the last thread; cut on the withdrawn thread line. Cover a backing board with fabric of your choice and position the sampler, pinning it at the centre and the corners. Stitch in place (a small curved needle may make this easier, with matching thread). Finally, carefully withdraw all threads at the edge to make a fringe, or make a hem if you prefer.

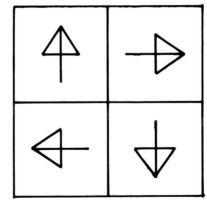

Above: Rotating the direction of the blocks

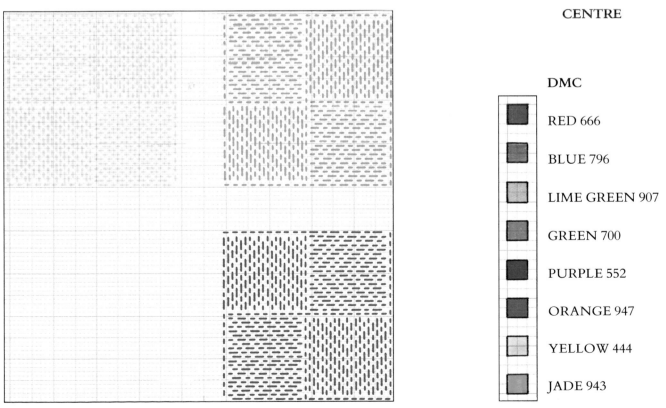

DMC

RED 666

BLUE 796

LIME GREEN 907

GREEN 700

PURPLE 552

ORANGE 947

YELLOW 444

JADE 943

MAP SAMPLERS

◊

For ornament and education

Many people believe that map samplers had a double function as both a medium for learning and displaying decorative needlework, and a way of teaching geography. The map sampler shown here is inscribed in stitch as being 'A Map of England and Wales'; though parts of southern Scotland and the east coast of Ireland are also shown. This map was one of the most popular with British embroiderers. Some maps were hand drawn (sometimes inaccurately) by young geographers, but by the 1780s map outlines commercially printed on to fabric were available, ready for embroidering. It was usual for embroidered maps to include the decorative embellishments shown on this sampler, such as the lavish floral frame and the points of the compass. Frequently the title of the map would be contained within a scrolling banner or floral framework. On more lavish examples the figure of Britannia would sit next to this embroidered title, and ships in full sail might be found around the coastline.

On this map sampler the counties of England and Wales have been outlined in coloured silk threads in stem stitch, and the name of each county is squeezed in in black cross stitches. Large counties such as Yorkshire provided ample space for this labelling, whereas little Nottinghamshire which lies beneath it presented a problem. Due to lack of space 'shire' has been abbreviated to SH in many of the counties. What is now called the North Sea this embroiderer has labelled the German Ocean; it is so-named in many map samplers of the period.

Some embroiderers concentrated just on a single county whilst others were rather more adventurous and stitched maps of European countries, the Continent and even the world. Such all-encompassing samplers as the latter could be worked in two ways: as two flat panels illustrating the continents between them, or three-dimensionally as a globe.

Although this sampler is worked on a woollen ground fabric, silk and satin materials were particularly popular for embroidered maps which depicted the entire world, either flat or in the round. In some cases the stitchery was confined to the use of black threads – presumably in imitation of the black lines and lettering on the printed maps. However, many more embroiderers had an evident love of colour and ornament, as shown here. The oval floral border has provided the perfect opportunity for decorative embroidery. Different periods favoured different flowers, and the flowers which meander around this map have a distinctly eighteenth-century appearance. However, it is technique as much as anything which makes these embroidered flowers characteristic of the 1700s. The map's floral border is worked in long and short and stem stitches: techniques which helped the embroiderer to illustrate her chosen flowers and plants as realistically as possible. Such attempts at naturalism, whether in coloured wool or silk threads, were a feature of much eighteenth-century embroidery. Elegant trailing plants, delicate floral sprays or more robust arrangements springing from vases, baskets and cornucopia were encountered on dress and furnishings. Consequently the counted-thread techniques which resulted in rigid, formal patterns were largely relegated to samplers, and with the exception of some whitework patterns and techniques, were not seen on fashionable dress. Because the map sampler was a very modern sampler form, (in the late-eighteenth century) these more up-to-date freestyle techniques and designs were preferred.

The embroiderer has garlanded her work with oak leaf and acorn sprays, daffodils, convolvulus, rosebuds and what may be either lilies or fuchsia. The convolvulus is a particularly popular eighteenth-century embroidery design choice, with the blue convolvulus flower popping up on many splendid eighteenth-century formal costumes and furnishings. The rose is an old favourite, but here it appears shaded and realistic as hairy moss rosebuds rather than as flat and stylised flower heads worked in counted thread techniques. Chenille threads were frequently used by late seventeenth- and eighteenth-century embroiderers to create a furry or fleecy texture, but in this sampler a much more unexpected material has been used. Look closely at the pale-pink rosebuds: the dark-green stems and calyx are actually made from bird's feathers which have been manipulated and stitched through the ground fabric.

The black threads used to label the counties and different seas have rotted and fallen away here and there. Frustratingly they have also fallen out of the cartouche at the base of the map where once they may have given the name of the embroiderer and date of her map.

The vogue for map samplers did not take off in America as it did in Britain, although some were produced across the Atlantic. The Society of Friends, or Quakers, appreciated the utilitarian value of this and the darning sampler and taught pupils at their schools to make them. The fine and detailed silk globe samplers worked at the Quaker Wesstown Boarding School in Chester County, Pennsylvania are often cited as exquisite examples of the finest Quaker-school embroideries. The names of terrestrial features or the planets were meticulously labelled in black ink or stitched with black silk threads to create impressively detailed globes.

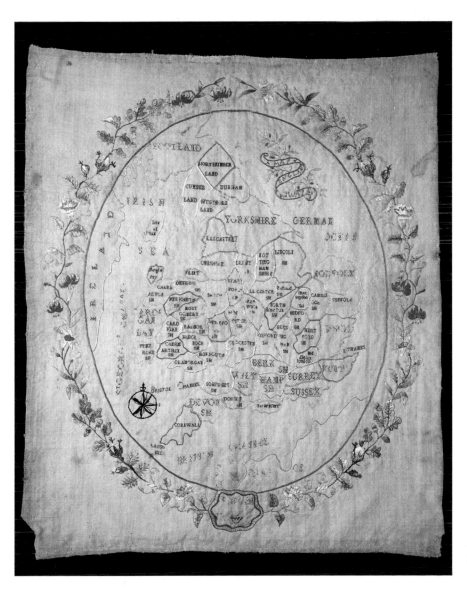

Late eighteenth-century map sampler showing the counties of England and Wales

OLD CRAY SAMPLER

◇

Designed by Pamela Warner

This sampler shows the church and other interesting buildings at Old Cray in Kent, and illustrates how buildings can be simplified, yet retain the essential features which make them recognisable. It also shows how to translate the buildings into stitches. The stitches used in the Old Cray sampler include split stitch, cross stitch, back stitch, French knots and pattern darning.

If you are a fairly experienced embroiderer, you may like to make a sampler of your own locality, adding personal touches, and adapting the instructions given below. Stitches can be added or omitted as you wish.

◇

Size (stitched area): 340 x 250mm (13¼ x 10in)
Materials
400 x 310mm (15½ x 12in) 26-count pale green Dublin linen

1 skein each of the following Anchor stranded embroidery cotton (floss):
grey 0397, 0399
golden brown 0367, 0369
blue 0130
green 0239, 0246, 0256
orange 0339
yellow 0301
pink 044
black
white

Tapestry needle 24
Crewel needle 8

1 Press fabric to remove creases. Mark the centre lines with tacking (basting) stitches to aid the positioning of the design. Transfer the design, see page 131.

2 Using the stitch guide below, follow the chart on pages 68-69.

3 Avoid taking dark threads across the back of the fabric as the colour may show through.

STITCH GUIDE

Outlines of the roads, lake and river: split stitch worked with two strands of embroidery cotton (floss).
Trees: French knots worked with three strands of embroidery cotton (floss) in a mixture of greens.
Grass: pattern darning worked over three threads and under one thread of the background fabric, using two strands of embroidery cotton (floss).
Buildings: cross stitch, worked over two threads of the fabric with two strands of embroidery cotton (floss), is used where solid colour is shown.
Roofs: pattern darning as for the grass.
Other outlines, small lettering and details of windows and gates: back stitch worked with one strand of embroidery cotton (floss). A sharp needle may be used on the diagonals to give a straight line.
Large lettering: cross stitch worked with two strands of embroidery cotton (floss).
Flowers and window boxes: small straight stitches worked with one strand of embroidery cotton (floss).

To make your own design
Find a map or street plan of your chosen place, and collect photographs or drawings of selected buildings. Make a note of the colours of the buildings.

With a black pen, take a simple tracing from the map of the main features – roads, rivers, etc. Adjust the tracing to the required size by photocopying, or by the traditional grid method (see page 131).

Also take tracings of the buildings or other items to be included. Leave out all small or unnecessary details which will be difficult to stitch. Adjust the size of these tracings in the same way as above, cut out the buildings and move them around on the basic map until you have a satisfactory arrangement. Pin or paste in position.

Take a tracing of the whole design and use this to transfer the outline to the background fabric, see page 131.

Old Cray Sampler, by Pamela Warner

THE BULL

THE BLUE ANCHOR

SURVEY HOUSE

ST PAULINUS

THE OLD CRAY

THE OLD STAR

THE MARY ROSE

ST MARY'S

OLD CRAY SAMPLER

CENTRE

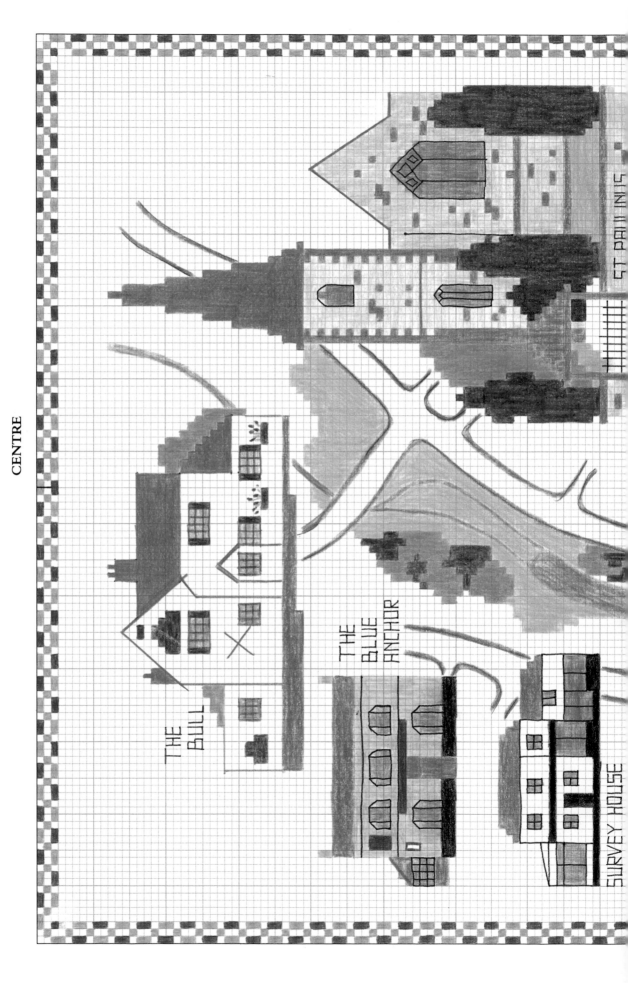

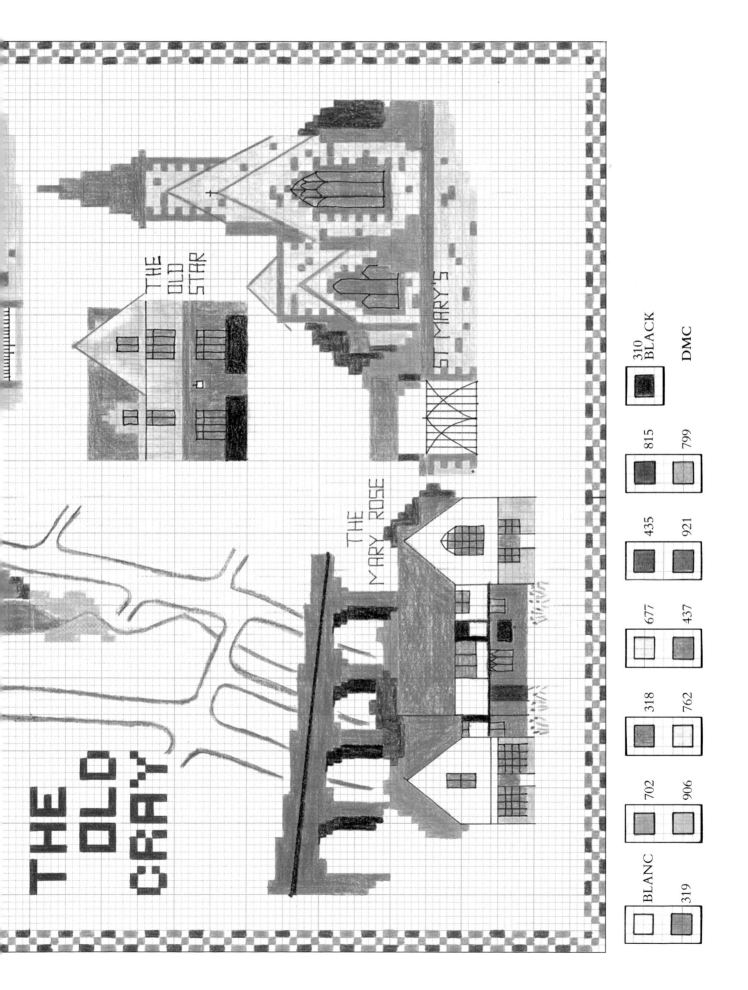

BIRD'S EYE VIEW OF A GARDEN

---◆---

Designed by Pamela Warner

This sampler, like the previous one, has taken its inspiration from the eighteenth-century map sampler illustrated on page 65. The ground plan of a modern house and garden includes the car in the garage, the tools in the garden shed and appropriate furniture in the rooms of the house. The garden is colourful with flowers. You could change some of the details, move things around and make a 'bird's eye view' of your own house and garden!

The sampler is an appealing one which you will find easy to work – most of the design is in cross stitch. Some French knots and pattern darning have been included to add interest, but cross stitch can be used throughout if you prefer.

Due to its simplicity, this sampler is an ideal beginner's piece and could well serve to introduce a young person to the delights of embroidery.

---◆---

Size (stitched area): 350 x 265mm (13½ x 10¼in)

Materials
450 x 365mm (17½ x 14¼in) 26-count cream Dublin linen
1 skein each of the following Anchor stranded embroidery cotton (floss):
white
pink 025, 088, 089, 096
gold 0279
yellow 0291, 301
green 0185, 0187, 0239, 0246
red 046
grey 0397
golden brown 0367, 0369
brown 0380
blue 0130
2 skeins each Anchor stranded embroidery cotton (floss):
grey 0399
green 0256
Tapestry needle 24

Work carefully from the chart. Each square represents one cross stitch. Variations to this are as follows:

STITCH GUIDE
The entire sampler can be stitched in *cross stitch*, worked over two threads of the fabric and using two strands of embroidery cotton (floss). Alternatively, the flowers on the bushes, plants and trees may be worked in French knots if desired.

The patches of grass are stitched in *pattern darning* over three threads and under one thread of the fabric, using two strands of embroidery cotton (floss). For beginners, cross stitch can be substituted if you wish.

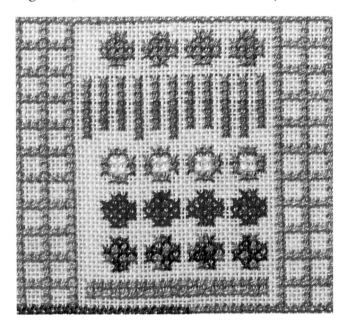

Detail of Pamela Warner's design

(right) Bird's Eye View of a Garden, by Pamela Warner

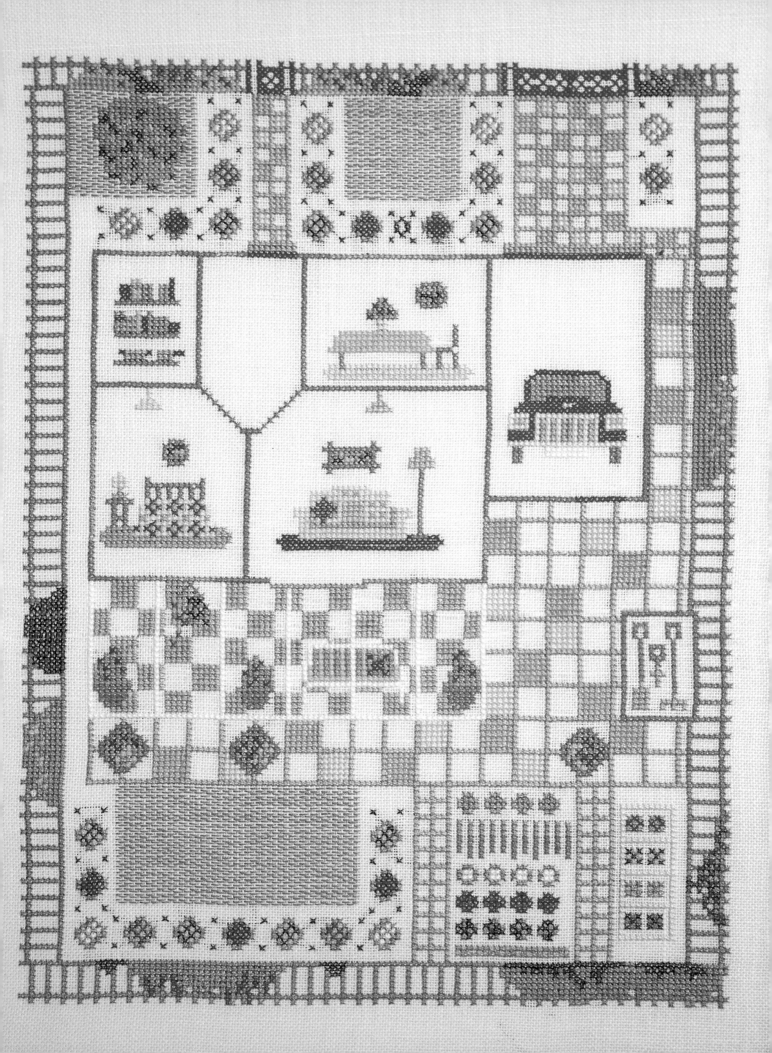

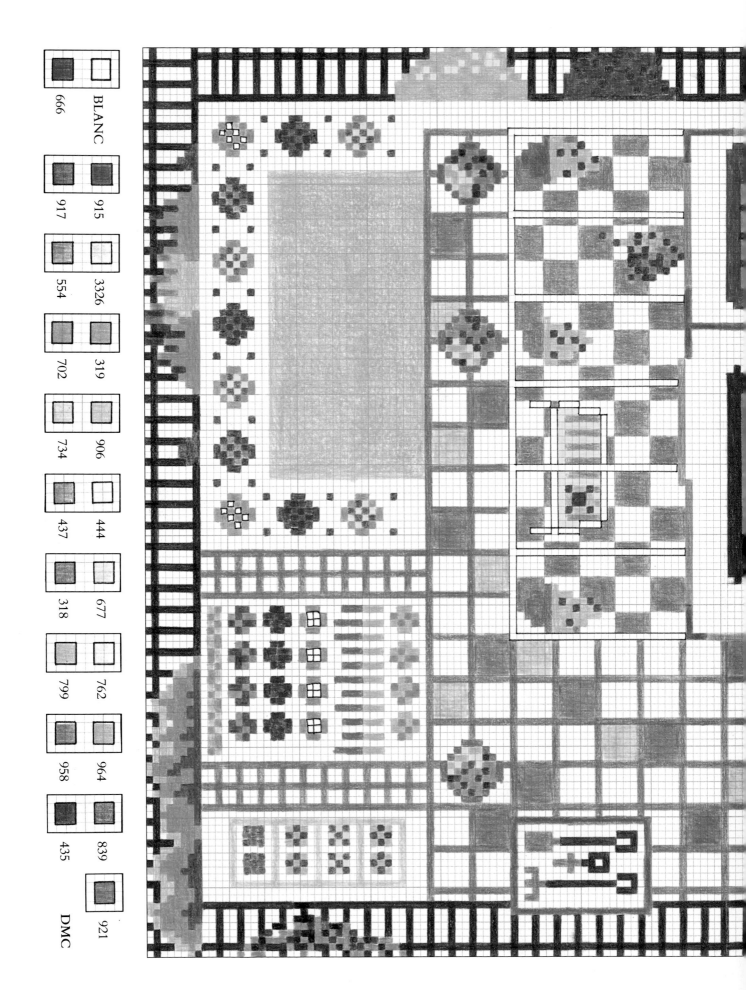

BLANC

□	■	
	666	

■	■	
915	917	

□	■	
3326	554	

■	■	
319	702	

■	■	
906	734	

□	■	
444	437	

■	■	
677	318	

□	■	
762	799	

■	■	
964	958	

■	■	
839	435	

■	
921	

DMC

BIRD'S EYE VIEW OF A GARDEN

CENTRE

ALPHABETS, BORDERS AND MOTIFS

A wealth of fancy forms

Many samplers were probably stitched primarily to be ornamental, whilst paying lip service to the notion of sampler making being an educational exercise. This sampler, which inspired contemporary embroiderer Brenda Keyes to create her piece *Decorative Lettering* on page 78, combines decorative embroidery with utility in the form of stitched alphabets. These alphabets are worked in particularly fancy forms which could not be easily copied in stitch or pen and ink.

The first band across the sampler is decorated with spidery letters worked in a combination of cross and running stitches. The second row of letters and the name Betty Clark (lower left corner) are worked in a form of cross stitch known as marking stitch, presumably because of its special use in marking fabrics with stitched letters and numbers for identification purposes. The crosses actually appear on the reverse of the ground fabric with letters being made up of a series of blocks on the surface. On this sampler the third and fourth interpretations of the alphabet (from A–K only) dominate. These letters in different forms are equally florid, being festooned with running stitched flourishes. The remainder of the sampler is decorated with motifs and band patterns and the whole is enclosed by a stylised strawberry-plant border, which by the close of the eighteenth century had become a popular and entrenched element in sampler design.

It is difficult to be precise about the date of this embroidery. Although it has many ele-

Late eighteenth-century sampler worked by Betty Clark; British

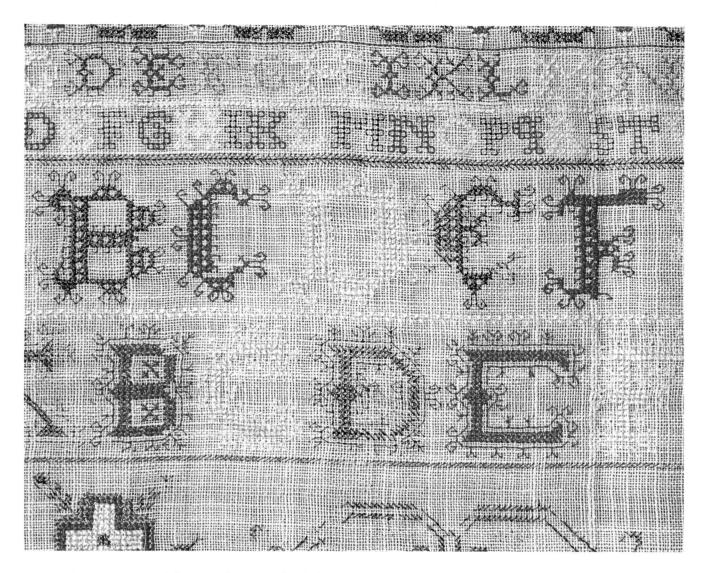

ments in common with samplers stitched during the 1780s and 1790s, a number of these features were confusingly carried on into early nineteenth-century sampler making. A telling omission is the absence of the letters J and U from the stitched alphabets. In most cases these do appear in sampler alphabets by the end of the eighteenth century; so their absence here suggests that this sampler was more likely to have been stitched during the years 1780–1800 than much later.

Look at the decorative elements more closely; the familiar stylised band patterns based on seventeenth-century models are prominently placed in this sampler. Beneath them is a band of motifs which were particularly popular with eighteenth-century sampler makers. These include dark-green tree motifs which have been 'clipped' into a desirable pyramid shape, and baskets holding piles of fruit (perhaps lemons?) piled symmetrically to a

point. The rather jaunty bird perched atop one of these is in contrast to the proud peacocks which are making fine displays of their colourful tails. If we look closely we can see that there are actually three of the smaller birds. The bird on the lemons is most visible since he has been embroidered in bright-pink threads, whilst the other two have been embroidered with threads of a barely visible cream colour. Look for them above the two small brown animals which look rather like rabbits, but may be stags (by the fruit baskets). Both these creatures, the jaunty bird and the stag, can be seen in earlier interpretations on seventeenth-century samplers. A very similar small bird motif is stitched discreetly among the lower band patterns on the sampler worked in 1680 by H.S. (page 23). Marion Glover featured this bird in her own work

This detail of Betty Clark's sampler clearly shows the bird, beast and plant motifs commonly found in eighteenth-century samplers

Songbirds and Carnations (page 27), where he can be seen more clearly. Look back to the sampler showing the clothed boxer figures on the Contents page; there is a variety of little birds and beasts in the lower part of the sampler. These include a lion (very difficult to make out), a unicorn and two stags. Heraldic beasts such as these were frequently embroidered on to samplers, though over the years the heraldic associations disappeared.

For interesting eighteenth-century comparisons look at the Ewart/Sawers sampler (page 45), and the one worked by Ann Richmond (page 52-53). You will find similar motifs in each of these; indeed the panel of mixed motifs just described here is very reminiscent of the two decorative panels embroidered across the

base of the Ewart/Sawers sampler. Here you will see clipped trees and birds, flowering plants, and stags very similar to those embroidered by Betty Clark. The little dogs with their curling tails (stitched in white coloured threads by Betty Clark and in black silk threads on the other two samplers) are very similar in all three. However Ann Richmond's stag is a prouder beast than the little mutant forms found in many eighteenth-century samplers, despite the fact that he has lost his antlers.

Betty Clark's sampler is worked almost entirely in silk thread on a linen ground. Metal threads were rarely used on late eighteenth-century samplers, but on this piece small amounts have been used to work the centre of two flower heads (the first two flowers on the left in the first band pattern below the alphabets). Perhaps the embroiderer was actually inspired in her work by a surviving example of an earlier embroidery glittering with gilt or silver gilt threads.

Project 11

DECORATIVE LETTERING

◊

Designed by Brenda Keyes

Many alphabets appear on samplers and some include extremely decorative capital letters. When Betty Clark worked the letters on her sampler in the eighteenth century (see page 76), she would have been amazed to learn that, two hundred years on, they would be the starting point for a twentieth-century sampler.

Besides beautiful capital letters, this sampler includes an alphabet and a number of decorative borders and motifs inspired by the original sampler. It also makes effective use of a limited number of stitches – cross stitch, back stitch, Algerian eye stitch, four-sided stitch and fly stitch. Not recommended for a beginner because it requires careful counting, the sampler will present no difficulty if you are already skilled.

The animals and birds in the bottom half of the sampler are charming. They could be re-arranged to make another sampler contained within one of the borders.

Brenda Keyes began her design with some ideas and samples

Decorative Lettering, by Brenda Keyes

Size (stitched area): 335 x 320mm (13 x 12½in)
Materials
460 x 460mm (18 x 18in) 25-count unbleached linen
DMC stranded embroidery cotton (floss):
orange 920
green 890, 935
red 3685
yellow 951, 743
pink 223
brown 780
ecru
Tapestry needle 24 or 26

STITCH GUIDE

1 The stitches used in this sampler are cross stitch, back stitch, Algerian eye stitch, four-sided stitch, fly stitch and tent stitch. Instructions for working the stitches will be found on pages 134-9. Unless otherwise stated, use two strands of embroidery cotton (floss) in the needle and stitch over two threads of the fabric.

2 Oversew the edges of the linen fabric to prevent fraying.

3 Fold the linen in half and then in half again to find the exact centre. Crease lightly. Work from this point outwards. If you wish, you can tack (baste) along the crease lines. These vertical and horizontal lines are indicated on the chart.

4 Carefully following the chart, work in cross stitch with the following exceptions:
Back stitch is used for thin decorative lines.
Algerian eye stitch forms the motif bottom centre, with the animal figure in ecru cross stitch.
Four-sided stitch is used for the letters of the smaller alphabet at the top of the sampler.
Fly stitch worked on its side makes the line underneath the smaller alphabet.
Tent stitch worked over *one* intersection is used to fill in the tiny birds which are first outlined with back stitch.

The line between the large letters at the top of the sampler and the smaller alphabet is worked in cross stitch, but the under stitch of the cross is worked in green 935 and the over stitch is worked in pink 223.

5 When the sampler is complete, stretch, if necessary, and mount (see page 132) before framing.

Decorative Lettering

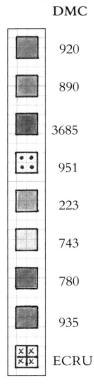

	920
	890
	3685
	951
	223
	743
	780
	935
	ECRU

CENTRE

INSPIRATION FROM BERLIN

A nineteenth-century craze

Berlin work, as the name indicates, was a form of canvaswork embroidery which originated in Germany. It was copied in simple stitches (usually cross and tent stitches) mainly in wools on to canvas from printed designs broken down into an arrangement of coloured squares. Each square on the charted design represented one stitch on the canvas. Berlin woolwork embroidery was eventually used to decorate a wide range of artefacts, including the catalogue of furnishings which were seemingly essential to mid nineteenth-century domestic comfort; for example fire screens, hand screens, bell pulls, pelmets, curtains and curtain ties, stool tops, cushion covers, rugs and carpets, table mats and runners. It was also used to create pictorial embroideries.

Bible stories and episodes from romantic literature of the day were frequently stitched in Berlin wools. The sentimental tone was continued in canvas-stitched representations of animals which were often domestic pets: the burgeoning royalist cult resulted in Queen Victoria's dog Dash being captured forever in cross stitch. More exotically, vibrantly plumed birds from foreign shores were transformed into plush-stitched dust traps. Plush stitch was the most technically demanding technique employed in Berlin work. This stitch, which was in vogue during the mid 1800s, was akin to rug-making techniques. It created rows of woollen loops, secured to the canvas by cross stitches, which were cut, brushed and clipped to create densely padded, contoured three-dimensional motifs.

A major advantage of Berlin work for the relatively unskilled embroiderer was the provision of ready made, easy-to-follow designs, the use of simple stitches and, as time went on, the easy availability of all required materials. Constructing a plushwork parrot may have presented an insurmountable problem to many women if it had not been possible to buy canvases with these parts already completed, or to engage professional embroiderers to carry out the more demanding work.

The two long, narrow Berlin-work samplers shown here were probably stitched by professional embroiderers and used to illustrate a range of stitch and design possibilities on offer to customers. Their length and narrowness is a particular feature of Berlin-work samplers, which like their seventeenth-century counterparts functioned as reference works, being rolled and stored when not in use. Such samplers carry an assortment of motifs and patterns which are often worked in a wider range of techniques than is usually found in amateur work.

The sampler signed and dated A. Karn 1847 includes a rather ruffled looking, plush-stitched budgerigar clinging to his perch with wire claws. This sampler is filled with examples of densely stitched patterns suitable for furnishings. The second sampler illustrates a collection of motifs and patterns, two of which demonstrate the combined use of contrasting materials. One example shows how satin ribbons can be secured by stitchery, whilst, in another, lengths of straw (here substituted by paper strips) are caught down by embroidery stitches.

The wools used in Berlin work can be easily distinguished from hard and shiny worsted wools. Sometimes silk threads were stitched in conjunction with the wools to provide highlights and during the 1850s and 60s the use of glass and metal beads became particularly

Typical long narrow mid nineteenth-century British Berlin woolwork samplers, and detail

popular with Berlin-work embroiderers. From the later 1850s the woollen yarns were dyed to vibrant hues using the newly developed chemical dyes. The lurid possibilities afforded by the new range of dyes had great appeal for the Berlin workers as their embroideries testify. On samplers such as these adventurous colour schemes can be eye-catching and inspiring.

Geometric patterns, narrative scenes, birds, animals and floral arrangements were all designs which could be purchased in chart form. The earliest charts were printed and hand coloured in Berlin, but as Berlin woolwork embroidery became internationally fashionable other countries began to produce the necessary charts. Eventually the hand-coloured charts gave way to ones coloured by lithographic printing processes. During the second half of the nineteenth century the use of such processes meant that full-colour printed Berlin-work charts could be issued with women's magazines.

The chart illustrated on pages 94 and 95 is inscribed with information which tells us where and by whom it was published: 'Berlin bei Carl J W Wicht Konigstr No 66'. The chart does not give the date of publication, but the restrained hand-painted design suggests that it was probably at some time from the early to mid-nineteenth century. In contrast, many of the floral designs issued later than c1840 depicted flamboyant flowers that were enviable, if not unbelievable in their large-scale magnificence. On the more modest designs seen here, the printed dotted outline of each wreath and the coded colour symbols can still be detected beneath the painted squares.

COLOUR AND PATTERN

◆

Designed by Janice Hay

This striking modern sampler sprang from a lively interpretation of the vibrant colours and zigzag patterns on the Berlin woolwork sampler on page 83. The inventive stitches, using a variety of threads, including silk, are worked on canvas which has been sprayed with gold paint. If this does not appeal to you, the canvas can be left unsprayed, but the effect will not be so rich. The sampler is fairly complicated, and will test your skills, but the unusual stitches are most intriguing. Small tassels add a final and unusual touch to the sampler.

The design is so adaptable it could also be used as the centre panel of an exotic silk or velvet bag or cushion. Large tassels at the corners of the cushion would carry the colours through.

◆

Size (stitched area): 140 x 150mm (5⅜ x 5¾in)
Materials
310 x 310mm (12 x 12in) 22-count mono canvas
1 can gold Humbrol mini spray paint
1 x 10g ball DMC pearl cotton in each of the following colours:
red 349(15), 498(4), 608(5)
blue 796 (8), 996(9)
1 x 2g skein of 20th Century Yarns Variegated Fine Silk in the following colours:
flamingo (1)   nutmeg (11)   amethyst (2)
damson (7)   pacific (14)
1 x 2g skein of Au Ver à Soie Stranded Silk in the following colours:
115(3)   134(6)   946(13)   1034(12)   1335(10)
40 x 25mm (1½ x 1in) piece of card for making tassels
Tapestry needle 24

A frame is not essential because the vertical and horizontal stitches do not distort the canvas. Spraying with gold paint also stiffens the canvas.

Where stitches are shown over stitches (with the exception of long diagonal stitches, see page 139), work vertical stitches first.

The chart shows the ground stitches only. Some long stitches have another thread wrapped round them using a contrasting colour (see page 85).

On the chart orange circles represent small French knots.

The row of stitches above the bands of amethyst long stitches is a variation of rice stitch, see page 137.

In some cases the stranded thread needs dividing. Use seven strands for outlining but fewer elsewhere as appropriate. Finer threads pass over thicker ones.

1 Spray canvas with gold paint (see page 131). Leave to dry.

2 Cut 465mm (18in) lengths of thread to work short stitches.

3 Measure 80mm (3in) down from the top of the canvas and 95mm (3½in) in from either the left or right-hand side and mark with a coloured thread. Start with a knot at the back. Work the amethyst (2) V-shape at the top, the single row of running stitches on the connecting strip, and continue across the design. NB The points of the V-shapes do not fall immediately under one another.

4 With flamingo thread (1) work the small triangles at the top.

5 Work down the design following the chart.

6 To finish, cut 515mm (20in) lengths for the long threads outlining the panels. Start at one corner and lay the thread to the next corner, take a back stitch into the back of the work and come up again in the same hole. Continue round each panel.

7 Use a single strand of contrasting silk to hold down the long threads with a cross stitch (see page 134) at 12mm (½in) intervals. 25mm (1in) can be left at the top.

8 Make eight small tassels (see page 85) using seven strands of silk: four in purple, two in pink and two in turquoise. Attach securely to top and bottom corners and along the bottom of the panel.

Small tassels

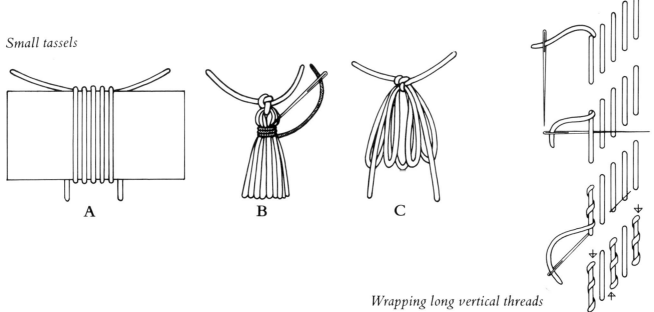

A   B   C

Wrapping long vertical threads

Colour and Pattern, by Janice Hay

HALF DESIGN TO BE MIRRORED MINUS CENTRE ROW

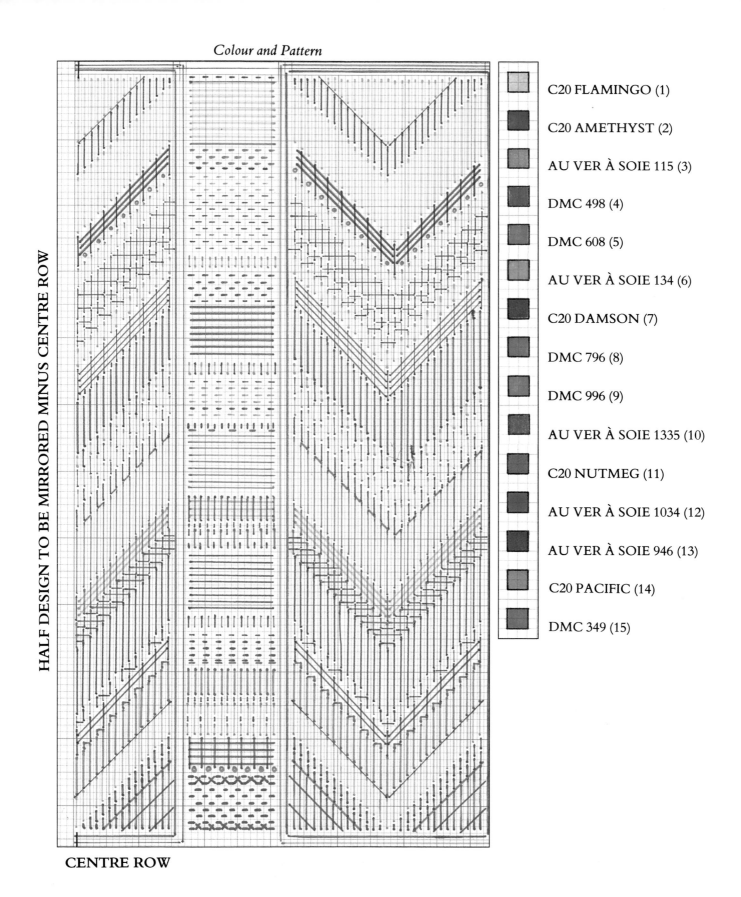

C20 FLAMINGO (1)

C20 AMETHYST (2)

AU VER À SOIE 115 (3)

DMC 498 (4)

DMC 608 (5)

AU VER À SOIE 134 (6)

C20 DAMSON (7)

DMC 796 (8)

DMC 996 (9)

AU VER À SOIE 1335 (10)

C20 NUTMEG (11)

AU VER À SOIE 1034 (12)

AU VER À SOIE 946 (13)

C20 PACIFIC (14)

DMC 349 (15)

CENTRE ROW

SAMPLER GREETINGS CARD

◊

Designed by Janice Hay

◊

Berlin woolwork of the nineteenth century inspired this richly coloured greetings card which, when it has served its purpose, can be framed.

Cross-stitch embroidery on perforated paper was also popular with the Victorians. Small triangles are worked separately and applied. This project is not suitable for beginners.

◊

Size (stitched area): 200 x 155mm (7¾ x 6in)

Materials

1 sheet 310 x 235mm (12 x 9in) red perforated paper

1 sheet 310 x 235mm (12 x 9in) gold perforated paper

Black or gold paper can be substituted for red but will give a slightly different effect.

1 x 10g ball DMC pearl cotton 8: pink 603(8), 553(14), red 608(12), 349(7), 498(5), orange 919(9)

*1 x 2g skein of 20th Century Yarns Variegated Fine Silk:
flamingo (3),
damson (11),
nutmeg (1),
poppy (10),
amethyst (13),
sorcery (15)*

*1 skein Anchor stranded embroidery cotton (floss):
purple 0112(4),
variegated red 1203(6),
1206(16)*

*1 skein DMC stranded embroidery cotton (floss):
green 943(17),
red 915(2)*

1 skein DMC coton à broder: red 304(5)

1 reel Madeira metallic machine thread FS 2/2 No. 20 gold

Most threads are interchangeable – see conversion chart page 140

Tapestry needle 24

360 x 230mm (14 x 9in) black card scored and folded to make the greetings card 230 x 180mm (9 x 7in)

PVA adhesive

Cut a piece of red perforated paper 113 holes down and 85 holes across. The right side is the smoother side. *Do not bend or fold the paper.*

Cut 460m (18in) lengths of thread. '2S' on the triangles chart means that two strands of stranded threads are required; 'D' means that a double thickness of pearl cotton is needed. Otherwise use the thread as it comes from the skein. Work from the background chart in a similar way; fine threads pass over underlying ones so that the colour shows through. Each square on the chart represents one hole in the paper. NB Spacing of zigzags and stitches is irregular – see chart. Where stitches are shown over stitches on the chart, work vertical stitches first (see page 139), except for long diagonal stitches. The chart shows ground stitches only. Many have metallic thread worked over them in another direction holding the long stitches close to the card, covering the holes. Work these as you go, and the long diagonal stitches between the rows last. Each stitch has two movements – from back to front and from front to back. Otherwise the paper will tear.

1 Begin with a knot at the back. Start at either the top left- or top right-hand corner using flamingo thread (3). Work across all 85 rows. Refer to chart and diagrams on page 89.

2 Work the three triangles at the top with nutmeg thread (1).

3 Fill the space between with thread (2), using all strands. Some stitches are vertical and some horizontal.

4 Continue working from the top down. Three rows of holes at the bottom give space to add a name and date if you wish.

5 The separate triangles are worked on gold perforated paper. Work the small stitches in the centre first, then the outer bands, followed by the edges. Use metallic thread to highlight between the rows on triangles B, C, E, F and G. Cut out along the row of holes next to the stitches. Triangles C and G have one empty hole at each bottom corner.

6 Stitch triangles in place on the background work, starting with A at the top. Each point slightly overlaps the triangle above. Starting at the back with a knot, take a matching thread through the card, make a stitch at each corner of the triangle, back through the card and fasten off. Do not pull too tightly.

7 To finish, mount the work on a slightly larger piece of gold perforated paper, using PVA adhesive. Then glue to the prepared black card. Alternatively, frame as a sampler.

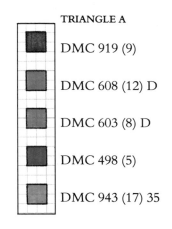

TRIANGLE A

DMC 919 (9)

DMC 608 (12) D

DMC 603 (8) D

DMC 498 (5)

DMC 943 (17) 35

TRIANGLE B

DMC 498 (5)

C20 AMETHYST (13)

DMC 603 (8) D

DMC 608 (12) D

TRIANGLE C

DMC 498 (5)

C20 FLAMINGO (3)

DMC 349 (7) D

DMC 943 (17) 3S

DMC 608 (12) D

TRIANGLE D

ANCHOR 0112 (4) 3S

DMC 553 (14) D

DMC 603 (8)

DMC 919 (9) D

DMC 498 (5)

DMC 943 (17) 3S

DMC 608 (12)

TRIANGLE E

DMC 498 (5)

C20 FLAMINGO (3)

DMC 349 (7) D

DMC 943 (17) 3S

DMC 608 (12) D

Sampler Greetings Card, by Janice Hay

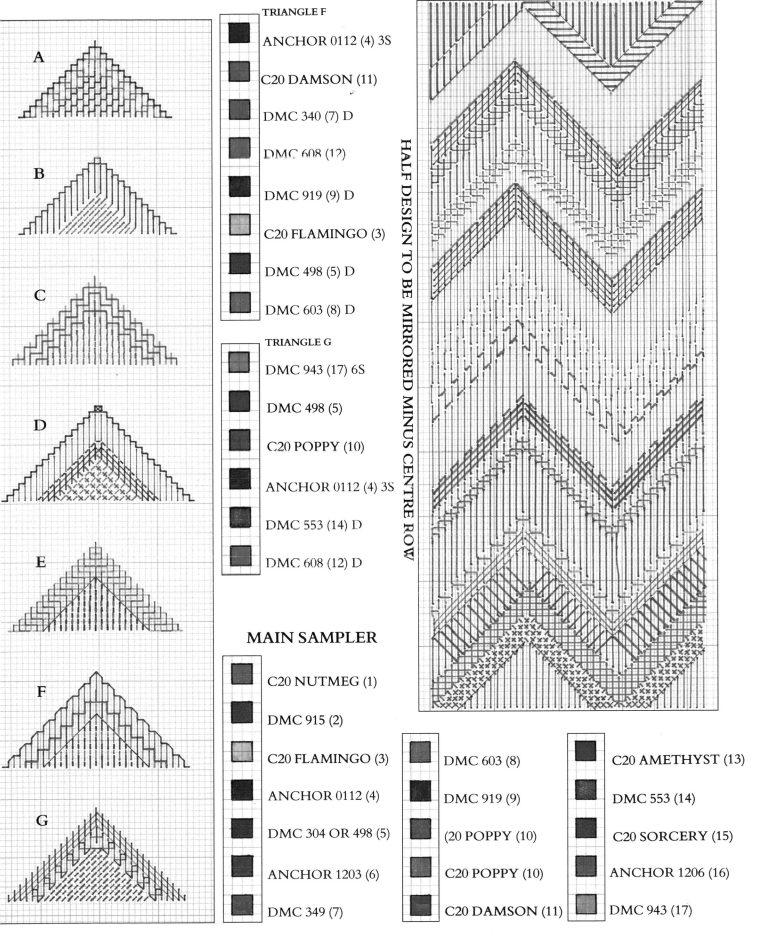

CENTRE ROW

A

B

C

D

E

F

G

HALF DESIGN TO BE MIRRORED MINUS CENTRE ROW

TRIANGLE F

ANCHOR 0112 (4) 3S

C20 DAMSON (11)

DMC 340 (7) D

DMC 608 (12)

DMC 919 (9) D

C20 FLAMINGO (3)

DMC 498 (5) D

DMC 603 (8) D

TRIANGLE G

DMC 943 (17) 6S

DMC 498 (5)

C20 POPPY (10)

ANCHOR 0112 (4) 3S

DMC 553 (14) D

DMC 608 (12) D

MAIN SAMPLER

C20 NUTMEG (1)

DMC 915 (2)

C20 FLAMINGO (3)

ANCHOR 0112 (4)

DMC 304 OR 498 (5)

ANCHOR 1203 (6)

DMC 349 (7)

DMC 603 (8)

DMC 919 (9)

(20 POPPY (10)

C20 POPPY (10)

C20 DAMSON (11)

C20 AMETHYST (13)

DMC 553 (14)

C20 SORCERY (15)

ANCHOR 1206 (16)

DMC 943 (17)

CONTRASTING TEXTURES

Designed by Vicky Lugg

A number of Berlin woolwork patterns have been arranged to make a sampler which focusses on contrasting textures. It also includes other ideas taken from Victorian canvaswork. Some of the stitches are worked over organza. Ribbons and beads are also included. The canvas is painted metallic gold and parts are left unworked. Although the colours are limited, the overall effect is one of richness and luminosity. It would be a most impressive gift.

The variety of materials and techniques employed make this sampler unsuitable for beginners.

Size (stitched area): 280 x 210mm (10¾ x 8in)

Materials

350 x 280mm (13½ x 10¾in) interlock canvas mesh 12, mounted in a rectangular (slate) frame

230mm (9in) square metallic gold silk organza

1 skein DMC pearl cotton 5:
yellow 676, 677
grey 415
ecru

1 skein DMC pearl cotton 3:
yellow 676, 677, 727
grey 415
beige 644
cream 712

DMC gold metallic thread Fil or Clair

Steff Francis hand-dyed threads: medium silk, medium-thick silk and viscose ribbon, all in gold/grey

Metallic ribbons: gold 7mm (5/16in) wide, silver 4mm (3/16in) wide

Small beads: clear and opaque, mixed golds and silver

Tapestry needles 18 and 22

Beading needle

String, medium-thick, 1.5m (5ft) approx

Deka permanent metallic gold fabric paint, or artist's acrylic paint

Paint the canvas evenly with gold paint using a fairly stiff brush. If necessary, thin the paint with water. Paint the string also and leave both to dry. Wash brushes at once.

Following the chart (overleaf) and colour illustration:

1 Work the outside border with straight stitch using medium-thick silk thread.

2 Couch gold ribbon inside the border with straight and cross stitches using pearl cotton 5/677, 415 and ecru. Cover four threads, starting at lower edge centre. Mitre the corners and overlap ribbon ends, covering with cross stitch. Fill the space between ribbon and border with back stitch in pearl 3/415.

3 Leave one thread space of canvas. Work a band of rice stitch on three sides of the square and part of the fourth side. Stitch over six threads with viscose ribbon for the underlying cross and pearl 3/712 and 727 alternately for the crossed corners. Additional corner stitches are worked with pearl 5/415 for the outer edge and ecru for the inner. Fine metallic thread makes the central crossing stitches.

4 Apply a square of organza to fit inside the rice stitch border. Tack (baste) in place.

5 Couch two bands of painted string with spaced straight stitches in ecru pearl 5★. Each band of string covers two threads. Start at the bottom, butt the ends of the string together and cover with stitches.

6 The 'interlaced' pattern is in cross stitch using pearl 3/677, 676 and 644; 727 and 415 are used for additional stitches. With matching thread, stitch a small gold bead in the spaces. Tack (baste) along the centre of each band as a guide. Remove tacking (basting) stitches later.

The rice-stitch border within the string fits round the corners of the central pattern. The cross is worked with pearl 3/676, over four threads; the crossed corners are worked in pearl 5/415. Accentuate the inner edge of this border with back stitch using pearl 5/676.

7 Fill the centre squares with gold and silver beads, plus some French knots worked with medium-thickness silk thread and pearl 3/676. The beads predominate in the centres.

8 With ecru pearl 5 and spaced straight stitch, apply two bands of silver ribbon, linking the central square to the lower edge. Each band covers two threads.

9 Diamond-shaped blocks of straight stitches in medium silk★ fill the area between the ribbons. One thread is left between the blocks, fill with diagonal lines of tent stitch in pearl 5/676

10 Stitch the side panels with bands of straight stitches in a wave pattern. Starting with the *top band left-hand side:* pearl 3/677, medium silk★, pearl 3/644, medium-thick silk, pearl 5/677★, two lines of medium silk★, pearl 5/676★

Right-hand side: pearl 3/644, medium-thick silk, three bands of medium silk★, pearl 5/677★, pearl 3/644, pearl 5/676★.

Finish the top edges of these panels with lines of back stitch in matching colours.

★take two stitches in each hole

Contrasting Textures, by Vicky Lugg

Contrasting Textures

Project 15

FROM A VICTORIAN CHART

◊

Designed by Rosemary Caie

Roses and auriculas were favourite flowers of Victorian gardeners and they blossom again as charming posies on this delightful sampler, based on the original Berlin woolwork chart (on pages 94–95) – the perfect complement to Victorian furniture and furnishings. The miniature wreaths and pretty border add further Victorian touches.

The soft colours echo those of the natural-dyed yarns in use in the early part of the nineteenth century, before chemical dyes were introduced. They would be at home in any room, and particularly in a bedroom.

In the language of flowers the rose symbolises love and Culpeper's *Herbal* tells us that the primula (of which family the auricula is a member) is under the dominion of Venus. Perhaps this sampler could become a gift intended to express affection?

The sampler is worked entirely in cross stitch over one thread of the background fabric, so the chart is reasonably simple to follow. The colours of the threads are as near as possible to the colours in the original Berlin woolwork.

◊

Size (stitched area): 290 x 215mm (11¼ x 8¼in)

Materials

500 x 420mm (19½ x 16¼in) antique white 14-count Aida

1 skein of DMC stranded embroidery cotton (floss) in each of the following colours:
green 500, 704, 905, 937, 3053, 3362
light blue/green 564
pink 335, 951, 963, 986, 3712, 3716
red 347, 814, 815
maroon 902
purple 327, 3042, 3740
brown 801
beige 842, 3032
grey 414, cream 677
golden yellow 973

Tapestry needle 24

1 If possible, mount the fabric in a rectangular (slate) frame, to keep the tension of the stitches even.

2 Tack (baste) a line *down* the exact centre of the fabric and another *across* the exact centre as a guide when counting threads to place the posies and the border. The guidelines must follow the thread of the fabric. It may also be helpful to take a tracing from the colour chart and mark the centres to correspond with the tacked (basted) lines on the fabric.

3 Starting at the top, and using one strand of thread in the needle, work each motif in cross stitch over one thread of the fabric in the colours indicated below, placing them as shown on the chart. Each square on the chart represents one cross stitch.

Top left: green 500, 704, 937; pink 335, 951, 3716; red 347, 815; maroon 902; brown 801.

Top right: green 500, 704, 937, 3053; pink 335; red 347; golden yellow 973.

Centre left: green 500, 704, 905, 937; pink 335, 963, 3716; red 347; maroon 902; purple 327, 3740; grey 414; cream 677.

Centre right: green 500, 704, 937, 3053; light blue/green 564; pink 986; maroon 902; purple 327, 3042.

Bottom left: green 500, 905, 3362; pink 3712; red 814; brown 801. *Bottom right:* green 500, 704, 905, 937; pink 3712; red 347; maroon 902; brown 801; beige 842, 3032; grey 414.

4 The border is worked in green 905, 937; red 347 and maroon 902.

Using the guidelines and counting carefully, start in the exact centre of each side and work outwards to the corners, repeating the pattern and working the corners as shown.

Berlin bei Carl F. W. Wich

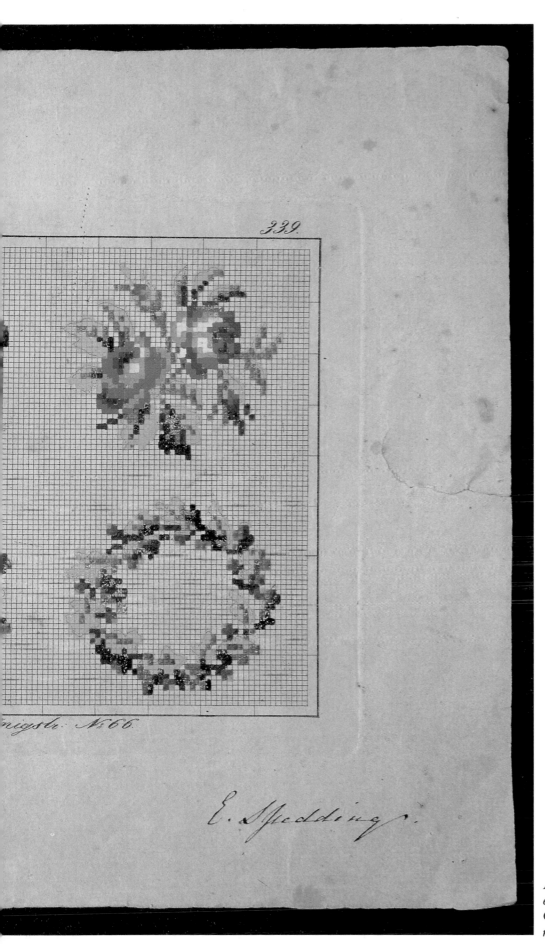

339.

nigsli: N° 66.

E. Spedding.

A chart for Berlin woolwork embroidery produced in Germany in the early-to mid-nineteenth century

From a Victorian Chart, by Rosemary Caie

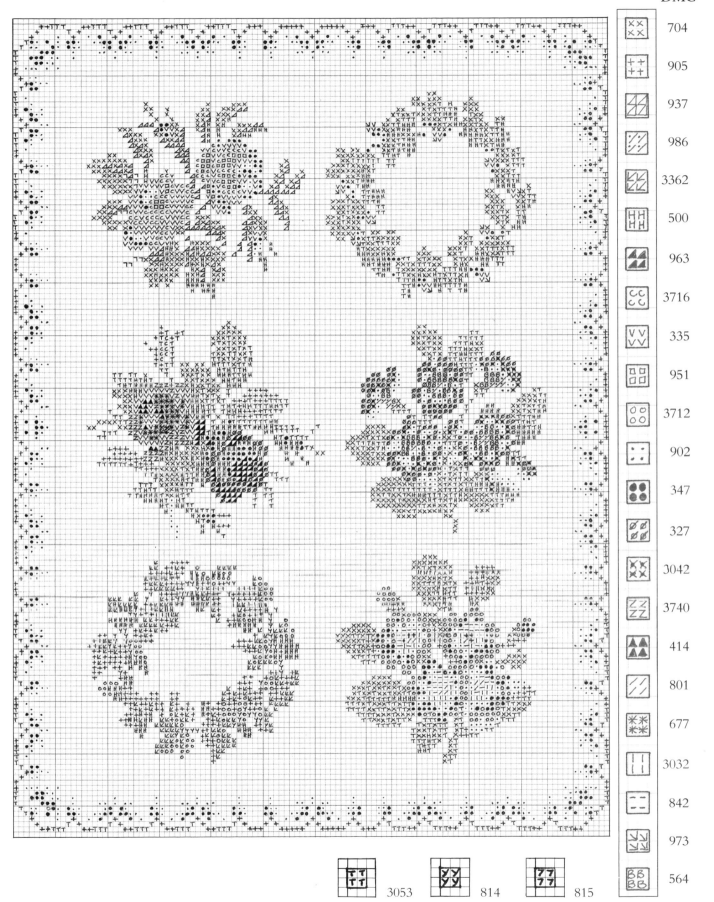

	DMC
XX / XX	704
++ / ++	905
▨	937
▨	986
▨	3362
HH / HH	500
◢◢ / ◢◢	963
CC / CC	3716
VV / VV	335
▦	951
oo / oo	3712
⠢	902
●● / ●●	347
⌀⌀ / ⌀⌀	327
XX / XX	3042
ZZ / ZZ	3740
▲▲ / ▲▲	414
▨	801
** / **	677
I I / I I	3032
-- / --	842
ϤϤ / ϤϤ	973
BB / BB	564

T T / T T	3053
yy / yy	814
77 / 77	815

ANIMALS AND BIRDS

◆

A Return to Familiar Motifs

This sampler, stitched in 1819, has a familiar feel. It includes a selection of patterns and motifs already seen in seventeenth- and eighteenth-century samplers in this book. The embroidered border which became a feature of eighteenth-century samplers is evident, and some of the individual motifs first met with in earlier samplers have been retained.

The figures which represent Adam and Eve standing on either side of a tree, and the rather mutant stags stitched at the top of the sampler are motifs which can both be found on seventeenth-century samplers, and are even more frequently seen on those worked in the eighteenth century. The houses, the carnations in vases and the perching birds were, by the early 1800s, traditional sampler motifs well known to embroiderers. Until the nineteenth century rabbits and cats were rather less common on samplers, particularly in the well-rounded form they take on this embroidery. Tortoiseshell cats like this pair with their distinctly well-fed domestic appearance make incongruous supporters of the central motif. This depicts the crucifixion, a subject which was rarely illustrated on British and American samplers before the nineteenth century. Rather more appropriate than the cats are the religious and moralising verses which are included in this sampler. They say:

> O love
> the Lord
> And he will be
> A tender father
> Unto thee
>
> Let virtue be my choicest care
> And Learning my delight
> To make the day completely fair
> And guild the gloomy night

The spelling is the embroiderer's own. These verses, which appear at the top of the sampler, are separated by the prominently stitched information that 'Hannah Gaunt finished this work in the 12 year of her age January 27 1819'. Perhaps if she had seen the remarkably minute and controlled stitchery of Mary Lucas (see page 13) our other 12-year-old embroiderer, then Hannah would not have been so willing to claim this embroidery as her own. These two samplers are markedly different in the levels of skill they exhibit, with Hannah by far the inferior embroiderer. She seems to have given little thought to the direction of her cross stitches: these are formed with the upper diagonal travelling from top left to lower right in some cases, and the reverse in others, giving a rough and uneven texture to the embroidery. Despite this, Hannah's sampler has its own charm, conjuring up a vision of a young embroiderer with rather more enthusiasm than skill and patience.

Certainly it is hard to imagine that many of the nineteenth-century samplers provided any opportunity for creative enjoyment. Many consisted of the alphabet, numerals, and doom-ridden verse stitched entirely in cross stitch. The amusement provided by selecting, arranging and stitching decorative motifs was excluded from the making of these serious samplers. In the majority of nineteenth-century samplers cross stitch is the predominant, and often only stitch used. The consequent association between samplers and cross stitch was probably responsible for this technique becoming known as sampler stitch, which is a term still encountered today. Cross stitch also happened to be a mainstay of Berlin woolwork, a type of embroidery which reached a peak of popularity in the 1850s.

Sampler worked by Hannah Gaunt in England in 1819

Detail of Hannah Gaunt's sampler showing one of a pair of embroidered cats

Floral motif on Hannah Gaunt's sampler

ADAM AND EVE

Designed by Patricia Sales

Bright colours and touches of humour make this attractive sampler a joy to embroider. It is based on Hannah Gaunt's sampler of the early-nineteenth century (page 99) which, with its appealing figures, animals and birds, has a very special charm. Some of the motifs have been adapted and used to make this contemporary version which will be appreciated by old and young alike.

The stitches are fairly simple. The motifs and most of the background are worked in tent stitch, with diagonal mosaic stitch for the dark blue background to add texture, depth and interest. Some of the surface stitches have been added after the background has been worked.

You do not have to use the stitches suggested, you can use any you feel would be suitable. This is your sampler – enjoy it!

Size (stitched area): 280 x 220mm (11 x 8½in)

Materials

435 x 360mm (17 x 14in) single canvas, mesh size 14 or 16

1 skein DMC stranded embroidery cotton (floss):
brown 3031
beige 612, 644
ecru
gold 729
terracotta 920
orange 720
blue 995, 3750, 3765
Scrap of vilene (pellon)
Indelible marker
Tapestry needle 18 or 20

1 Draw outer dimensions of the sampler on to the canvas with the indelible marker. Carefully count the threads and mark the centre of the design.

2 Use six strands of embroidery cotton (floss) and begin by working the motifs, including the border. Work out from the centre, counting threads as you go.

3 Use tent stitch throughout. Each square on the chart represents one tent stitch. The apples on the tree are not worked now but are stitched on top of the background threads when the rest of the work is finished.

4 When the motifs are complete, outline the sections of the sampler. The inner rectangle is in terracotta, the outer rectangle in brown. Lay down long threads from corner to corner, taking the ends

through to the back of the work (tramming). Cover these lines of thread with straight Gobelin stitch to give a padded effect. Use double thread in blue 3765, and a thicker tramming thread, to outline the whole sampler.

5 Work tent stitch in blue 3765 for the background which extends beyond the terracotta outline and partly behind some of the motifs. The remaining background up to the brown outline is worked in diagonal mosaic stitch with dark blue 3750 to add texture and interest.

6 Now you can add the surface embroidery stitches. The designer used raised picot stitch for the leaves of the tree, Adam's and Eve's leaves and the mouse's ear. Padded satin stitch worked over a small piece of pelmet-weight vilene (pellon) was used for the apples. See page 132.

The stems of the leaves are made with detached overcast stitch, and the cats' features and birds' legs with back stitch, with the addition of French knots.

Adam and Eve, by Patricia Sales

ADAM AND EVE

CENTRE

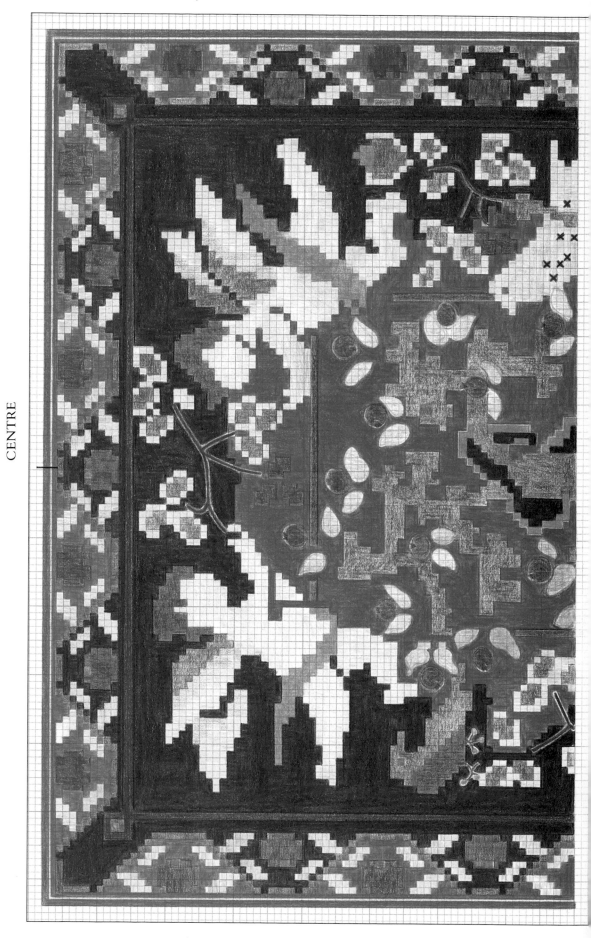

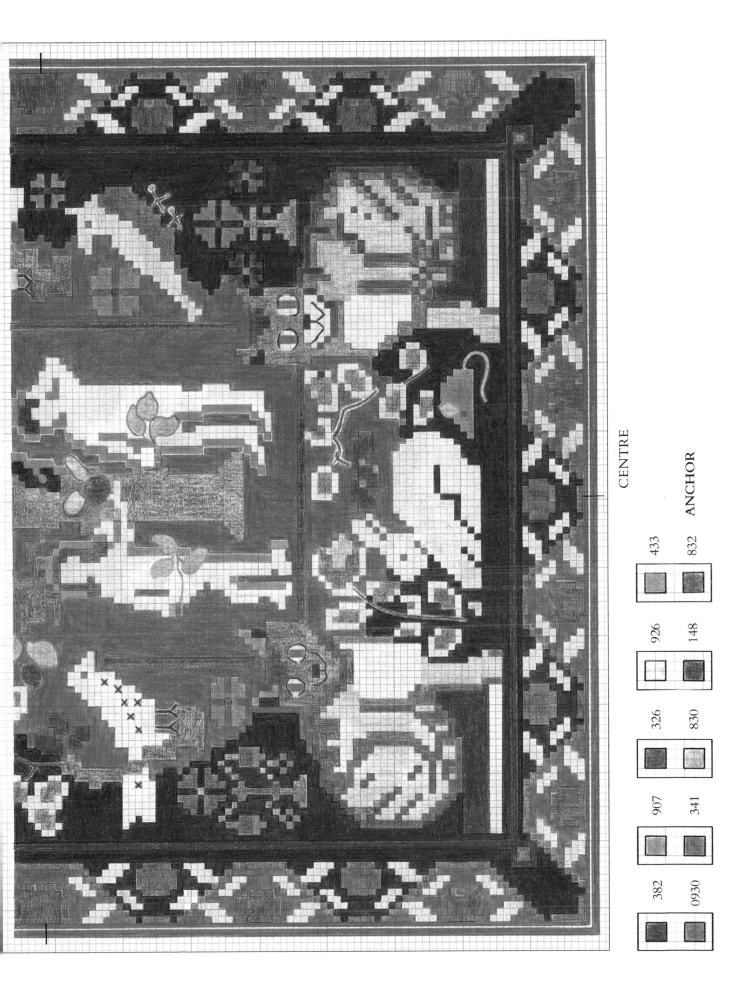

CENTRE

ANCHOR

382	907	326	830	926	433
0930	341			148	832

CRAZY PATCHWORK

Alternative style – a rich record of Victorian life

By the beginning of the nineteenth century the young domestic embroiderer stitched her sampler more as a leisure pursuit, and as a requirement of social convention, than as a reference work of embroidered designs. As the 1800s progressed, sampler making as an entertainment or mark of female accomplishment waivered in popularity amongst the wealthy whilst the stark alphabet, numeral and plain-sewing samplers continued to be stitched by less affluent children who attended charity and Board schools. However, throughout the nineteenth century embroidery remained a leisure pursuit of prime importance amongst the growing population of affluent women with much 'free' time but little enough to fill it. As the decades passed, different embroidery techniques and styles came in and out of fashion. During the mid- to later-nineteenth century the obsession with Berlin work subsided, and the vogue for alternative types of needlework developed.

A variety of rich and sometimes unusual materials were put to use to create an assortment of weird, wonderful and often unnecessary objects. Patchworking became a popular pastime. The many surviving examples of pieced fabric hexagons, diamonds and blocks remain as glowing albums of the materials available at the turn of the nineteenth and twentieth centuries. This crazy patchwork cover provides a particularly rich record of late Victorian dress and furnishing fabrics. The jumbled arrangement of fabric shapes is evidently the origin of the name for crazy patchwork, but the irregular composition itself is said to have been influenced by Japanese designs. The relatively small size of this piece suggests that it was not made as a full-scale bed cover but was probably intended as a decorative throw for a bed or sofa, or perhaps even as a tablecloth.

The patchwork is made up of twelve pieced blocks which frame a central square. Plain and patterned silks and satins, brocades, ribbons, velvets and plush fabrics have all been included in the work. Not content with the decorative effects of these contrasting fabrics, the maker of this cover has embellished her work with a profusion of embroidered motifs. Some of these, which are machine stitched, have been cut from their original background fabrics to be applied to this patchwork; many more have been directly hand embroidered in silk threads.

Browsing through the blocks is an absorbing exercise which results in a long list of the different motifs and stitches used. Many of the motifs are flowers (including roses, pansies, tulips, fuchsias, fruit blossom and daisies) but – more unusually – simple chairs, pocket watches, fan shapes, anchors, a teapot, a cat's head, a key, a neo-classical tomb and human figures are also found. Whether or not these had a special meaning for the embroiderer is unknown, but certainly several of the motifs show the influence of decorative styles then in vogue.

During the later nineteenth century an influx of Japanese artefacts had an influence upon European fine and decorative arts. In the patchwork, vestiges of this are recalled in the use of 'oriental' motifs such as the blossom sprays, butterflies, fan shapes and chrysanthemum-like flowers. Amongst the motifs an embroidered peacock feather recalls the textile design by Arthur Silver entitled *Peacock Feather*. This exotic design made famous as a Liberty's printed textile in the late 1880s is now almost a hallmark of the period, evoking as it does the love of opulence and exoticism which also created our sumptuous patchwork cover.

This glorious patchwork cover is typical of work made between 1880 and 1900

CRAZY PATCHWORK 'SAMPLER'

Designed by Jo Verso

Schoolgirls once learned the basic embroidery stitches by sewing a sampler. Each stitch was worked in a uniform line on a strip of linen and, when finished, the sampler was rolled up and placed in a drawer where it languished indefinitely. It is much more stimulating to learn the stitches by embroidering a piece of crazy patchwork – the 'lesson' will be a richly exciting one in terms of colour and texture and the product will be worthy of display.

The pattern given here is a guide to such a project, but it allows complete freedom to substitute individual fabrics and notions. Choose embroidery threads and beads to tone with the available fabrics, and, where appropriate, adapt the patches to your level of skill and the materials to hand.

Size: 172 x 177mm (6⅝ x 6⅞in)

Materials

300mm (12in) embroidery hoop
360mm (15in) square of calico (muslin)
Scraps of silk or cotton fabric (the original used dark, medium and light purple, violet, shocking pink, dark blue, bluey mauve, turquoise, bluey green, blue/green/purple stripe)
Scrap of gold net (optional)
Scrap of dark-blue organza (optional)
4 mother-of-pearl buttons
3 small star-shaped sequins
Assorted seed, bugle, gold and silver beads
Assorted sequins
1 shisha mirror
1 decorative heart- or leaf-shaped bead
Short length of fine ribbon
Scrap of gold sequin waste
Tacking (basting) thread, sewing thread, metallic threads (Madeira Gold Metal Effect Yarn 5012 and Madeira multi-coloured metallic machine embroidery thread were used on the original)
Short length of decorative, slubbed knitting wool
Stranded cottons (floss) in colours to tone with the patches
Mulberry medium- thickness silk threads (optional – some were used instead of stranded cottons (floss) on the original)
Beading needle (for beads)
Assorted sizes of crewel needles for the embroidery

1 Trace the complete design on to tracing paper. This will be laid over the work as it progresses to check accuracy.

2 Take another tracing of the design (seam lines only) to make a pattern for cutting the fabrics. Cut out each pattern piece.

3 Pin the pattern pieces to the chosen fabrics and cut out each patch, adding 25mm (1in) seam allowance all round.

4 Trace designs 3, 5, 10 and 14 on to their respective patches. For recommended method of tracing see page 131.

5 Prepare patch 16. Cut a piece of gold net to fit and tack (baste) it over the patch (optional). Alternatively use a patterned fabric for this patch.

6 Prepare patch 13. Stitch beads and sequins to the patch and cover with a piece of organza (optional).

7 Assemble blocks of patches as in Fig 1. Join patches by placing them right sides together and seaming with a fine running stitch. Trim the seam to 7mm (¼in) and press the seam towards the darker of the two patches. Continue until all the blocks in Fig 1 have been assembled. Lay the tracing of the complete design over the blocks to check that the work is accurate. When all five blocks are complete join block B to block C in a similar fashion, then add block D.

Crazy Patchwork 'Sampler', by Jo Verso

8 Cut a piece of calico (muslin) 380 x 380mm (15 x 15in) and mount into a 300mm (12in) embroidery hoop.

9 Tack block BCD to the calico (muslin), then lay block E right sides facing over it and seam the two together as before, but stitching through the patches and the calico (muslin). Trim the seam, turn the block to the right side and tack down the loose edges. Add block A in the same way. Use the tracing to check that the patches are lying in their correct positions.

10 Decorate each patch as follows. Use stranded cotton (floss) to work bullion bars, stem, satin, lazy daisy and long and short stitches. For other stitches metallic thread or Mulberry medium silk thread can be used.

Complete design

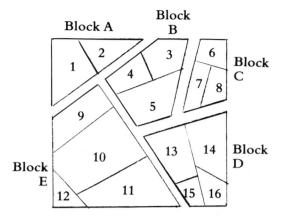

Blocks of patches

11 Using the coloured illustration as a guide, decorate the seams with the following stitches: herringbone stitch, Cretan stitch, straight stitch, feather stitch, chevron stitch, buttonhole stitch, closed buttonhole stitch, chain stitch . . . or whatever takes your fancy.

Patch 1: Bullion bars; French knots.
Patch 2: Cut a piece of sequin waste to fit the patch. Catch it down with straight stitches and stitch seed beads into each hole.
Patch 3: Stem stitch; satin stitch.
Patch 4: Thorn stitch; long-legged French knots.
Patch 5: Work the butterfly's body in satin stitch, couch the feelers. Work split stitch around the outline of the wings which are then worked in long and short stitch. If this is too daunting, work the butterfly in stem stitch in the same way as the violet (patch 3) is worked.
Patch 6: Couching.
Patch 7: Attach a shisha mirror, surround it with buttonhole stitch and long-legged French knots. Alternatively, the shisha mirror can be replaced with a shiny button surrounded by stitching.
Patch 8: Using metallic thread, stitch on a decorative bead.
Patch 9: Stem stitch; lazy daisy stitch. Attach buttons using beads if desired.
Patch 10: Satin stitch; stem stitch; lazy daisy stitch.
Patch 11: Couch lengths of decorative, slubbed knitting wool to the patch using one strand of gold thread and Cretan stitch.
Patch 12: Attach three star-shaped sequins using metallic thread and straight stitch.
Patch 13: Add some more sequins and beads to the surface of the organza to give a layered look to the patch. Alternatively, omit the organza and stitch sequins and beads to the basic patch.
Patch 14: Bullion bars; stem stitch; lazy daisy stitch.
Patch 15: Twist a length of ribbon into a bow shape and hold in place with French knots.

Applying shisha glass

Detail of the original patchwork cover showing the placing of fabrics in a 'crazy' arrangement with embroidered motifs

WESSEX EMBROIDERY

◆

A wealth of yearning verse

Margaret M. Foster of Bath was designing and stitching her own distinctive embroideries during the early decades of the twentieth century. Her 'little sampler for the month of May' is a typical example of Wessex stitchery – the embroidery which she developed. It could be that this term was suggested by the Saxon name for the area in south-west Britain in which she lived, or perhaps it referred to the design of her embroideries.

Margaret Foster gave names to some of her patterns, and often these were taken from geographical locations, e.g. the Lindisfarne pattern and Steep Holm (named after islands off the coast of Britain). The Lindisfarne pattern, which is worked in back, satin and overcast stitches creates an all-over flower-like design very similar to one embroidered on the sampler shown here (third band from the base).

Although the inspiration which lay behind many Wessex stitchery designs is not definitely known, one Wessex panel in existence is decorated with a familiar pattern; the stylised strawberry border frequently seen on samplers stitched at any time between the seventeenth and nineteenth centuries.

Many of the stitched patterns recall the similarly detailed designs and meticulous stitchery of Tudor and early Stuart blackwork embroidery. The piece shown here is set out in the manner of a seventeenth-century sampler which emphasises the nostalgic references which are such a feature of Wessex stitchery. However, whereas blackwork embroideries were monochrome works with perhaps some metal thread highlights Margaret Foster used a wider, though distinctive palette: pale blues, pinks and red, yellow and beige tones were her preferred thread colours, used on white or cream-coloured ground fabrics.

At first glance her all-over patterns of crosses, stars and rosettes appear to be regular throughout, but a longer look at some pieces reveals subtle changes in thread colour and stitched details. In her own words Margaret Foster described how these variations emerged from her working method: 'A Wessex needle . . . asks for no suggestions for pattern or design on paper or material; it can even produce good effects without any previous planning of the workers thought and brain, for it has stitches of its own by the use of which patterns will as it were evolve themselves . . .'

The variation in pattern and shifts in tone created by her spontaneous way of working gave some of her finished embroideries a degraded or worn look, which again is reminiscent of aged work.

The Wessex embroideries emphasise the passage of time, evoking a transient world rather than one of solid permanence. This is heightened by the stitched inscriptions. This one, and another wartime Wessex sampler in the Embroiderers' Guild Collection carry particularly poignant lines which record the armistice of 11 November 1918. The following is a transcription of these lines, set out approximately as they appear on the sampler:

A little sampler for the
month of May work'd
while skies were warm and
flowers were gay And all
good British people humbly
pray'd that Peace with
Victory be not delay'd

4th yr of the
grt war

designed & work'd in
May 1918 M.M.F.

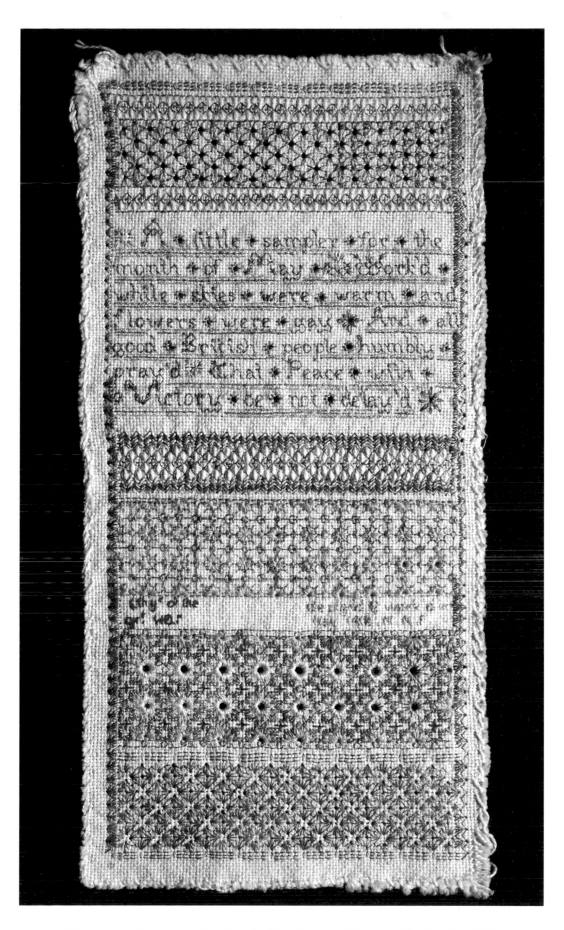

Wessex sampler designed and worked by Margaret Foster in England in 1918

WESSEX STITCHERY

◊

Designed by Moyra McNeill

In this design some of the stitched patterns which characterise Wessex embroidery have been grouped to make a stylised tree form, an appropriate accompaniment to the quotation from W. B. Yeats' poem *The Lake Isle of Innisfree*. The 'tree' gives the impression of shelter, peace and stability.

The stitches of the open repeating patterns, worked with fine threads, are pulled tightly to make small holes – another characteristic of

Wessex embroidery. To emphasise this the sampler could be backed with colour or with reflective metallic paper when finished. The style of the lettering is similar to that used on the original Wessex samplers.

The sampler is worked mainly in back stitch, with some straight stitches, so it is not a complicated one if the chart is followed carefully. You may like to choose your own colours in which to work it.

◊

Size (stitched area): 230 x 170mm (9 x 6½in)
Materials
500 x 400mm (20 x 16in) 25-count evenweave fabric
1 skein Anchor stranded embroidery cotton (floss):
red 0335
yellow 0298
dark blue/green 0851
Tapestry needle 22

1 Fold the fabric in half in each direction and crease. Mark the crease line with tacking (basting), making sure it is on the grain. This will be removed when the work is finished. Use a colour which cannot be confused with the embroidery threads.

2 Mount the fabric in a round or rectangular (slate) embroidery frame to make it easier to count the threads. It can be tricky to count threads diagonally, so count along the grain horizontally and then up or down.

3 All the patterns are worked with two strands of embroidery cotton (floss). To keep an even tension easily, thread a single strand about 700mm (27in) long in the needle and fold it over; do not use too long a thread because it will knot and wear in the eye of the needle.

4 All lettering is counted over one thread of the fabric and is worked with one strand of thread. One line on the graph represents one thread of the fabric.

5 To begin, make a knot in the thread and take it through the fabric to the back, leaving the knot on

the surface about 80mm (3in) from the first stitch. When several stitches have been worked, the knot can be cut off and the thread woven into the stitches at the back. Begin and finish all other threads by weaving into the stitches at the back in this way.

6 Because it is necessary to tension the stitches, use back stitch wherever possible. Pull the stitches tightly to make holes. Begin stitching at the centre point of the fabric, where the two tacked (basted) lines cross. First, work the trunk of the tree downwards, following the chart. Complete one vertical row of the pattern at a time.
NB Unlike cross stitch, the patterns are not counted over the same number of threads all the time, so follow the chart carefully.

7 Complete the trunk, then the flowers at its base. The foliage of the tree consists of bands of patterns. Begin at the centre and work outwards. (If you prefer, you can select one pattern and work all the foliage in that). The 'dropping leaves' are segments of pattern in a random arrangement.

Wessex Stitchery, by Moyra McNeill

WESSEX STITCHERY

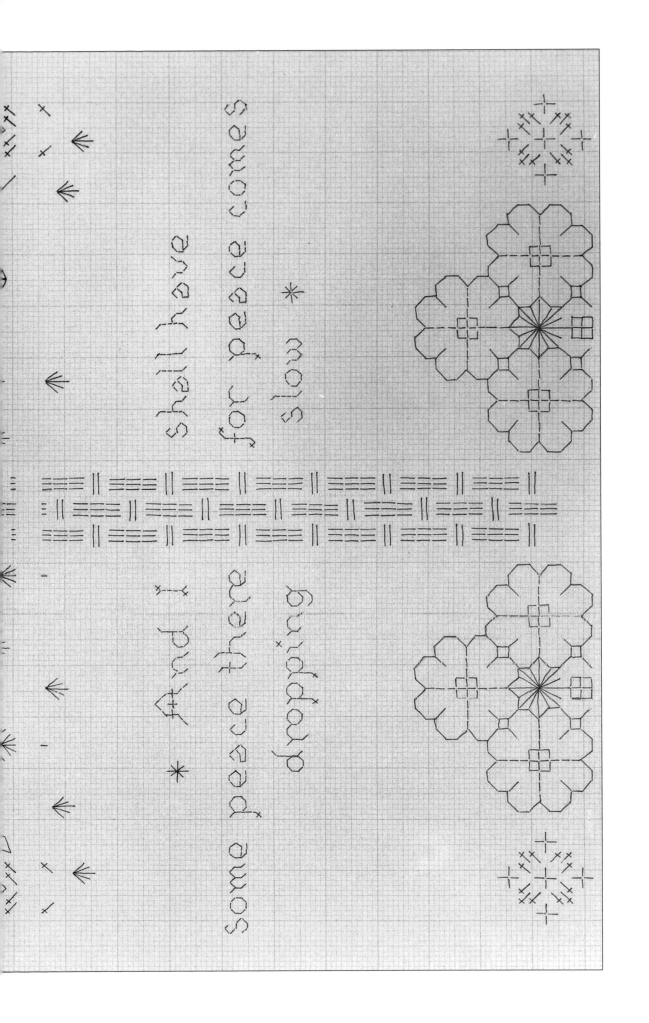

WAYSIDE FLOWERS

◇

A sampler from the early twentieth century

Early twentieth-century embroideries often recall the needlework of earlier times, particularly the skilled vital work of the sixteenth and seventeenth centuries. Technical excellence was held in great esteem by many embroiderers at the beginning of our own century; so it is not surprising that they should take the lively, yet meticulously worked Tudor and Stuart embroideries as their models or source of inspiration.

Joan Drew (1875–1961) was an embroiderer and teacher with a well-developed respect for historic embroidery which showed clearly in her own work. She used her skills to create and decorate costume pieces, banners and furnishings which employed the traditional materials and hand techniques well loved by embroiderers during the early twentieth century. Some of these appliquéd, quilted, smocked and hand-embroidered pieces survive now in the Embroiderers Guild Collection. Amongst them is this little, narrow, stitch sampler. The debt it owes to seventeenth-century embroidery is evident. The use of a length of linen to demonstrate a collection of stitched patterns immediately recalls the band samplers which were embroidered during the 1600s as records of stitch and design.

As with many of the earlier embroiderers, Joan Drew reserved a section of her sampler to record individual, or spot, motifs: in this case a choice of flowers, and as became the custom during the later seventeenth century she has signed and dated her work in stitchery.

Her selection of flower motifs are wayside or meadow flowers: the buttercup, viola, daisy and forget-me-not. They are amongst the plants known to the Elizabethans; similar humble flowers are recorded in herbals and literature of the time and survive to this day as embroidered decoration skilfully stitched in linen, silk and metal threads on sixteenth- and seventeenth-century costumes and furnishing pieces. These modest blossoms also appealed to many embroiderers earlier in this century, who either incorporated them into new designs in an Elizabethan style, or faithfully copied the original flower embroideries from the period.

Joan Drew admired historic embroidery and drew inspiration from the past. However, she did not advocate slavish copying from existing work, or reliance on commercially produced patterns. Rather, she had very strong feelings about the creation and use of original designs. In 1929 she published *Embroidery and Design* which she called a 'People's Book of Embroidery'. Through it she hoped to inspire, instruct, and to encourage embroideresses (she envisaged all embroiderers as female) to 'depend upon her own efforts of brain, eye, and hand, rather than upon the machine-printed embroidery patterns of the factory, that are turned out by the thousand'. Her book was liberally illustrated with designs which she hoped would stimulate the reader and act as 'stepping stones for the march of their own gifts of ingenuity and invention'. Every one of the motifs or patterns in it is based upon a plant or flower transformed into a stylised design suitable for interpretation through embroidery. The flower motifs on this sampler are typical of those illustrated in Joan Drew's book.

This sampler, featuring wayside flowers, was worked by Joan Drew in England in 1918

FLOWERS AND PATTERNS

◆

Designed by Sheila Miller

lowers and patterns combine to make this delightful sampler, a most acceptable gift for a friend. The colours can be changed to suit any decor.

The original early twentieth-century sampler by Joan Drew (page 119), on which this design is based, makes use of a charming pattern of flowers to illustrate a variety of stitches. This idea is repeated in the border design of wild flower heads surrounding a miniature sampler of simple stitch patterns. Fine threads give an air of delicacy to the stitches, which are not difficult to work.

The design is an adaptable one. Quite a different effect can be achieved by working the border entirely in white on a coloured background fabric with the stitch patterns in a deeper tone of the background colour. The stitch patterns can also be worked in white or a contrasting colour, or in a mixture of colours. Alternatively, the panel of stitch patterns shown could be worked on a larger scale to make another sampler.

◆

Size (stitched area): 180 x 120mm (7 x 4¾in)
Materials
390 x 350mm (15 x 13½in) closely woven linen or cotton fabric. (The cotton and linen mixtures sold for surface embroidery are ideal)

390 x 350mm (15 x 13½in) washed medium-weight calico (muslin)

DMC stranded embroidery cotton (floss):
light purple 554
mid purple 552
deep purple 550
light green 3348
mid green 3346
light yellow 744
mid yellow 742
blue 793
rose red 3350

Crewel needle 9 or 10

1 Make a tracing of the design.

2 Transfer to fabric using one of the methods described on page 131. Make sure that the vertical and horizontal lines of the border match the vertical and horizontal threads of the fabric.

Alternatively trace and cut out flower shapes in thick paper or fine card. Draw lightly round the shapes, directly on to the fabric, using a fine *permanent* drawing pen, first outlining the border with tacking (basting) stitches as a guide. An original design can be made in this way, planning it on paper before transferring it to the fabric. The flower shapes should be overlapped as in the original and should completely fill the border.

3 Tack (baste) guidelines for the stitch patterns in the centre of the panel following the weave of the fabric.

4 Stitch the calico (muslin) to the back of the surface material and mount in a rectangular (slate) frame (see page 132) to aid stitching.

5 Stitch through both fabrics using one strand of thread throughout the border. Two threads can be used to emphasise some of the stitch patterns.

Stitch patterns
1: fly stitch.
2: chain stitch.
3: 2-way buttonhole stitch and fly stitch.
4: chain stitch and French knots with zigzag chain stitch at the apex of the chevrons.
5: Cretan stitch and fly stitch worked sideways and crossed.
6: buttonhole stitch threaded with herringbone stitch and laced.
7: buttonhole stitch, chain stitch and fly stitch.
8: satin stitch and chain stitch.
9: fly stitch and star stitch.

Flowers and Patterns, by Sheila Miller

FLOWERS AND PATTERNS STITCH GUIDE

Border
A: satin stitch
B: buttonhole stitch
C: chain stitch
D: Cretan stitch
E: fly stitch
F: French knots
G: stem stitch

Patterns for floral border and flower shapes

Detail of Joan Drew's sampler showing flower motifs

INSPIRATION FROM MEXICO

◊

Bold and vivid – a Mexican sampler

The bold use of colour is the immediate attraction of this nineteenth-century Mexican sampler. After the Spanish conquest of Mexico (1521–1821) embroidery in that country evolved under many influences: indigenous Mexican, imported Spanish, European and Chinese materials and decorated textiles have left their mark. The rainbow patterns seen here are a feature of many Mexican samplers, also to be found in Spanish and some European pieces. Not surprisingly, since Mexico was a colony of Spain for three centuries, Mexican samplers are similar in design content and layout to Spanish samplers. A format favoured by Spanish sampler makers was to arrange patterned bands in concentric squares. This arrangement can also be found in Mexican samplers. Rectangular samplers were an alternative in both countries; this sampler is composed of a square of cotton divided into two rectangular panels.

Several of the band patterns seen here are familiar from their use over centuries on many European samplers; in particular the stylised plant and flower patterns (top left panel) which were originally derived from sixteenth-century pattern books. Whilst printed patterns were scarce in colonial Mexico, embroidery designs and motifs were more likely to be distributed within the country in the form of samplers and already decorated textiles. Indeed, samplers were important teaching aids and reference works of fashionable embroidery designs and techniques.

Surviving Mexican samplers date from the late-eighteenth century onwards, and as with this sampler they display motifs and band patterns drawn from European sources. These samplers are invariably of a notably high technical standard. Some of them carry names and dates and were probably produced by wealthy girls and young women as a demonstration of a genteel accomplishment just as they were in Europe. There must have been others, particularly before the nineteenth century, which were stitched as training exercises and kept as reference works by professional embroiderers. Indian workers were banned from some craft guilds during the colonial period, but were allowed to operate as textile workers because of a pressing need for home-produced textiles. Also, Indian girls as well as the daughters of wealthy colonists were taught European embroidery skills and designs in convent schools. Inevitably, European techniques and fashions will have been adopted and adapted for use in indigenous textile designs and costume traditions.

This nineteenth-century sampler, which is in the European tradition, is worked throughout with floss silk threads: a material favoured by both Mexican and Spanish sampler makers. Originally the threads seen here were a stronger colour. Today they have faded somewhat, but the patterns they make are still vividly attractive.

The boldness of the designs can disguise the skilled way in which technique and colour have been used to create subtly shaded patterns. This is particularly so in the geometric patterns arranged down the right-hand panel of the sampler. The tonal changes which occur in the purple silk embroidered pattern (left base corner), however, are not due to the intricacies of technique, but are simply because the fine silk threads have rotted and begun to fall away.

This surface-satin stitched pattern and the one embroidered above it are both similar to patterns seen on Spanish samplers of the nineteenth century and much earlier. Many of the bands embroidered here are carried out in drawn threadwork, a popular technique on nineteenth-century Mexican samplers. Again it is an element of Mexican embroidery inspired by a European tradition: drawn threadwork has been used for centuries by European embroiderers to decorate costume pieces and secular and ecclesiastical furnishings. The stylised plant patterns seen here are worked in this technique: the motifs have been left in solid relief against a gridwork of threads wrapped in

This nineteenth-century Mexican sampler clearly shows the influence of European patterns

coloured silks. The adjacent geometric patterns have been embroidered by withdrawing many of the ground threads and skilfully manipulating the remaining warp and weft filaments with silks to create complicated patterns.

The bands shown here also feature needle-weaving, satin stitches and Florentine work. Although they are not used on this sampler, reference to other Mexican samplers will show that motifs worked in free-style embroidery techniques and contrastingly controlled cross-stitched designs can also be found.

Detail showing some of the band patterns in the Mexican sampler

Project 20

MEXICAN ADVENTURE

◊

Designed by Willemien Stevens

The rainbow-coloured Mexican sampler was the inspiration for this adventurous modern design (page 128) using dyes, bonded appliqué and free machine stitching. It brings up to date the concept of the sampler as a means of recording experiments and ideas for future reference. The layout of the sampler is an echo of the seventeenth-century band samplers.

The use of a swing-needle domestic sewing machine may be surprising but, if you have one and are experienced at using it, you will not find this particularly daunting. You may need to practise the suggested method of applying the patterns if it is new to you.

Easy-to-use fabric dyes which can be fixed with a hot iron are now readily available in small jars. The colours suggested are approximate as it will be difficult to match the original colours exactly. This will make your sampler unique!

The motifs are ironed on to the background using Bondaweb, a fusible fabric, the textile equivalent of double-sided tape (you may have used it for dressmaking). The motifs are then outlined with free satin (zigzag) machine stitch. There are a number of excellent books available which give advice on framing work for free machining and the technique itself. Your public library should be able to help you.

The restrained colour of this contemporary sampler ensures that it will harmonise with the decor of any room.

◊

Size (stitched area): 340 x 230mm (13¼ x 9in)

Materials

500 x 400mm (20 x 16in) medium-weight calico (muslin)

Scraps of thin silk: pink, dark pink, golden/beige, blue, yellow, cream, dark green and gold; satin: pink or mauve. If you do not have fabrics in these colours, they can be dyed with transfer dyes, see below

Thread: Madeira Stitken No 30K, colour beige 1060

Bondaweb

Sewing machine needle 100

Deka fabric dye for silk ochre 765

Deka iron-on (transfer) dyes: pink 474, blue 479, black 488, green 483, lemon yellow 471. You may not need some of these dyes if you have coloured fabric scraps, see above

Round embroidery frame

1 Thoroughly wet the calico (muslin).

2 Mix a small amount of Deka ochre silk dye with a little water. Sponge some dye evenly over the calico (muslin) and leave to dry. This is your background fabric.

3 Working from the top down, each 'band' of the sampler is dyed individually with iron-on (transfer) dye. Dilute the dyes with a little water and paint the 'bands' on to computer paper or similar:

Band 1 pink 474
Band 2 blue 479 and a little black 488 mixed
Band 3 black 488 diluted to make grey
Band 4 green 483
Band 5 blue 479
Band 6 lemon yellow 471 mixed with a very little black 488

When the dyes are dry, place the paper face down on the dyed calico (muslin) and iron to transfer the coloured bands to the background. It is now ready for the patterns to be applied.

4 Trace the patterns on to the Bondaweb, and iron on to your chosen silk or satin fabrics. Cut out the patterns carefully, remove the backing from the Bondaweb and iron on to the appropriate 'band', placing them as shown in the colour illustration.

5 Mount the sampler in the ring frame so that the reverse side rests flat on the bed of the machine. Keep the fabric very taut. Lower or cover the feed dog (according to the make of your machine), remove the foot, and set the machine to the zigzag stitch. Rest your hands on either side of the frame and begin to stitch, slowly at first and with control. This may need practice. *Take care that your hands*

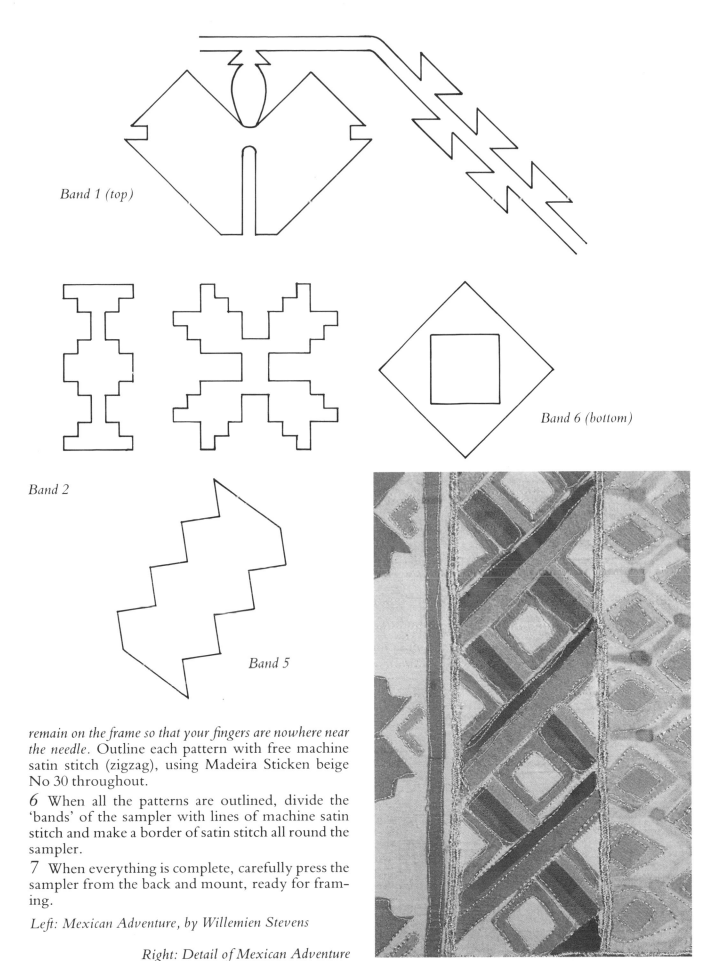

Band 1 (top)

Band 2

Band 6 (bottom)

Band 5

remain on the frame so that your fingers are nowhere near the needle. Outline each pattern with free machine satin stitch (zigzag), using Madeira Sticken beige No 30 throughout.

6 When all the patterns are outlined, divide the 'bands' of the sampler with lines of machine satin stitch and make a border of satin stitch all round the sampler.

7 When everything is complete, carefully press the sampler from the back and mount, ready for framing.

Left: Mexican Adventure, by Willemien Stevens

Right: Detail of Mexican Adventure

BASIC TECHNIQUES

◆

Equipment

You will need a sharp pair of scissors for cutting canvas and fabrics. They should not be used for any other purpose, particularly not for cutting paper which soon blunts them. A pair of small embroidery scissors is also useful.

Use a thimble if you can – it has many advantages, not least that it saves wear and tear on the fingers. If you are working two-handed (see below), you may find it helpful to wear a thimble on each hand.

A tapestry needle is the most suitable for canvas-work and counted work on linen, Aida, etc. It has a long eye and blunt end which will not split the threads of the background.

Frames

As you will have seen from the instructions given for the projects in this book, the use of an embroidery frame is often recommended. Not everyone likes to use a frame, but it does a great deal to prevent distortion of the canvas caused by the diagonal pull of many stitches. If a frame is used it may not be necessary to stretch the work when it is completed. A frame also helps to keep the tension of the stitches even, which gives the whole sampler a better finish.

A circular frame (also called a 'ring frame', or 'tambour frame' because it is used for tambouring – a type of embroidery worked with a tambour hook) is not suitable for use with stiff canvas. It may mark the work and it is not possible to stretch the canvas tightly enough. However, this type of frame can be used for working on even-weave linen, or fabrics such as Aida which are not so stiff.

It is a good idea to bind the inner ring of a circular frame with soft fabric. Bandage, tape or bias binding are all suitable. This acts as padding and prevents marking the embroidery fabric. Avoid trapping any stitched parts of the design already worked between the rings as it may be difficult to remove any marks so made. Removing the frame between working sessions will also help to avoid this.

A circular frame is used for free-style machine embroidery and the inner ring of the frame must be bound as described in the previous paragraph. In

this case it helps to keep the fabric taut and in contact with the foot plate of the machine, which is essential for this particular technique.

Rectangular embroidery frames, sometimes referred to as 'slate frames' or 'tapestry frames', are suitable for most kinds of embroidery, including work on canvas. Some are provided with floor stands which makes it possible to work with two hands; one hand remains on top of the work and pushes the needle through the canvas; the other hand stays below the work and returns the needle through the canvas ready for the next stitch. This speeds up the work considerably and is a skill worth acquiring, although it may need some practice. Alternatively, the frame can be rested against a table or between the backs of two chairs, but this is not so comfortable as using a floor stand.

Rectangular frames consist of a roller at top and bottom, each with a piece of webbing attached along it, and two slats which form the sides of the frame. The length of the webbing on the rollers dictates the maximum width of canvas which can be worked on a particular frame. Before making an expensive purchase, check that the tape is as long, or longer, than the width of the canvas to be mounted on the frame. The slats are screwed to the rollers or slotted through them to form a rectangle which can be adjusted to various sizes. If the depth of the canvas or fabric is greater than the depth of the rectangle, the surplus can be wound round one of the rollers. As the work progresses, the stitched canvas can be wound round the opposite roller with a piece of soft fabric or some acid-free tissue paper inserted to protect it, and more plain canvas unwound and brought into use.

To 'dress' a frame

1 Turn in a 12mm (½in) hem at the top and bottom of the background canvas and mark the centre of each with a thread or indelible pen.

2 Also mark the centre of the tape on each roller of the frame.

3 Match the centre of one end of the canvas to the centre of one roller and firmly stitch the two together, working from the marked centre outwards. Then repeat with the other end of the canvas and the other roller. Be sure to keep the hem underneath and the tape facing outwards on both ends at all times.

4 Stitch a length of tape along each side of the canvas to protect and strengthen it.

5 With very strong thread or thin string, lace the sides of the canvas to the side slats of the frame. To do this, fasten the thread securely to the frame at the point where one of the slats meets the roller, then take a long stitch through the canvas and back round the slat before taking another stitch. Continue in this way, keeping the stitches approximately 40mm (1½in) apart. Lace the opposite edge of the canvas to the other slat in the same way.

6 Pull the thread or string so that the tension is even on both sides of the frame and the canvas is stretched drum-tight. Fasten off the lacing by securing it to the frame. The frame is now ready for working your embroidery. As you work the canvas will probably become slack. When it does, undo the lacing, adjust the tension and secure the lacing again.

Transferring Designs

Most of the samplers in this book are worked from a chart, but in one or two cases the design needs to be transferred to the background fabric. The methods for this are outlined below.

Embroidery transfer pencil

1 Make a tracing of your chosen design using a black indelible pen or felt tip and a large piece of tracing, greaseproof or layout paper. Turn the tracing over and accurately go over the lines of the design with an embroidery transfer pencil.

2 To transfer the design, place the tracing in the centre of your fabric (the side with the transfer pencil downwards), leaving a good margin all the way round. Iron with a medium-hot dry iron. Press evenly all over, paying particular attention to the edges. As a precaution against scorching, protect any exposed fabric with more paper.

Tissue paper method

1 Trace the design on to tissue paper.

2 Place the tracing over the background fabric and tack (baste) along the tracing lines.

3 Tear away the tissue paper carefully, leaving the stitched outline of the design on the background. The stitches can then be removed as the work proceeds.

Window method (Use this method for *Crazy Patchwork 'Sampler'*, page 108)

1 Tape a tracing of the design to a window during daylight.

2 Place the patch over the tracing and tape it in place also.

3 Using a finely sharpened pencil, carefully trace the design on to the fabric. On dark fabrics use a white crayon.

Enlarging and Reducing Designs

Designs worked from a chart can be made larger or smaller by using canvas or fabric of a lesser or greater count. The higher the count number, the smaller the image will be; the lower the count number the larger it will be. By working small samples and counting the number of stitches per 250mm (1in), you can estimate the size a design will be when worked on canvas of different gauges.

Traditional method of enlarging or reducing any design

1 'Frame' the design with a pencil square or rectangle, then take a tracing of it.

2 Using a ruler, draw a grid of equally spaced vertical and horizontal lines over the tracing (the design will now look as if it was drawn on enlarged graph paper). Give each vertical and horizontal line a number so that the lines and squares can be easily identified.

3 On another sheet draw a second grid in proportion to the first – larger if the image is to be made bigger, smaller if it is to be made smaller. The second square or rectangle must contain the same number of squares in both directions as the first grid.

4 Drawing freehand, transfer the design to the second grid, square by square.

Photocopying is a quick and simple way of enlarging or reducing a design. Printed on to graph paper of the required gauge, it produces a ready-made chart.

Preparation, starting and finishing

Spraying or painting the canvas
The contemporary samplers *Colour and Pattern* (page 84) and *Contrasting Textures* (page 90) are both worked on canvas which has been coloured metallic gold.

The canvas of *Contrasting Textures* is brushed with metallic-gold fabric paint and left to dry.

The canvas background of *Colour and Pattern* is sprayed with metallic gold paint. It is essential to work in a well-ventilated room or, if it is a still day, you could work outdoors. Spread plenty of newspaper out around the spraying area, and place the canvas in the centre. Wear rubber gloves and protective clothing. Shake the can as instructed on the label, and work in short, sharp sprays, rather than continually. You need only spray the canvas on one side. Allow to dry for at least 24 hours.

Warning Keep away from children and pets. Follow all normal safety precautions regarding naked flames.

Preparing your canvas or fabric

1 If using fabric other than canvas, press to remove any creases.

2 Fold fabric into four and gently crease along the fold lines.

3 Tack (baste) along the creases. The point where the lines cross at right angles corresponds to the exact centre of the design. This is a great help when counting from a chart.

If you are using canvas, carefully count the threads in both directions to establish the position of the centre line, and mark with tacking (basting) stitches as above.

3 Unless specified otherwise in the instructions, work from the top of the design to the bottom, or from the centre outwards, whichever feels the most comfortable. In the same way, start borders in the middle of each side and work outwards.

4 Use short lengths of thread, approximately 300mm (12in). A longer thread will wear thin as it continually passes through the background, giving the surface an uneven appearance.

5 Start with a strong knot at the end of the thread and take the needle through to the back of the canvas or fabric a little way from where the first stitch is to be made. Position the thread at the back so that the first stitches cover and secure it. When it is secure the knot can be cut off and the thread run in at the back of the work.

Successive threads should be started in the same way. It is tempting to begin with a knot at the back, but knots can make the finished work look lumpy.

6 Finish by running in the surplus thread through the back of the stitches for about 25mm (1in).

7 If you have to take dark threads across the back of the work, check that they do not show through on the right side.

If you are using a stranded thread, cut short lengths, remove the number of strands you need, and smooth them so that they are not twisted. If any thread twists while you are stitching, let the needle drop and the twist will unwind.

Padding

The sampler *Flowers with Strawberries* (page 18) includes two methods of padding some of the motifs to raise them from the surface. In the sampler *Adam and Eve* (page 102) the first method is used.

Padding buds with thick vilene (pellon)

1 From the vilene (pellon) cut out the oval shape of the bud.

2 Tack (baste) in position with a cross stitch in the centre to hold it firm.

3 Cover the oval shape with satin stitch, beginning in the middle of the motif and working first towards one end and then to the other. This makes it easier to work.

Padding for the lower strawberry

1 Cut a piece of felt to the size of the motif, a second slightly smaller, and a third smaller still. Starting with the smallest shape, sew in position with stab stitches. Place the second-largest shape over the first and sew that down too. The largest shape goes over the other two and is also stitched down. This makes a smooth domed shape for the padded base which is then covered with stitches.

Stretching and Mounting

Stretching

If there is any distortion of the canvas, the finished embroidery will need to be stretched. To do this:

1 Place some layers of newspaper, topped by one or two layers of *white* blotting paper, on a wooden board. They should be larger than the work to be stretched. Damp them thoroughly and evenly.

2 Rest the embroidery on top, face up. Using rustproof drawing pins, carefully stretch the work to its correct shape and make sure the background threads are 'square'. Working out from the middle of the top edge, securely pin along the outer edges of the canvas or fabric. Keep the pins about 25mm (1in) apart. Pin the bottom edge in the same way, and then the sides.

3 Leave the embroidery to dry out naturally for several days. It can then be removed from the board and will be ready for mounting. If there is still some distortion, it may be necessary to stretch it again or seek professional advice.

Mounting

1 First decide the size the panel or sampler needs to be when mounted ready for framing. It may look better with some plain fabric left round it. Tack (baste) a guideline round this area. Allow a further 50mm (2in) of canvas or fabric all the way round for turning in.

2 Cut a piece of stiff acid-free card the size of the tacked (basted) area.

3 Place the embroidery face downwards on a clean surface with the cut card resting on it inside the tacked (basted) area.

4 Fold back the surplus canvas or fabric at the sides over the card and, using a very strong thread or thin string, take long stitches from one side to the other (lacing), working from the centre outwards. Pull the stitches tightly and check the front of the sampler every now and again to make sure it is correctly positioned.

5 Fold back the surplus canvas or fabric at top and bottom and lace in the same way as the sides. The long stitches will cross the previous ones more or less at right angles. It may be necessary to trim away a little surplus canvas or fabric at the corners in order to make a neat fold. The sampler is now ready for framing.

A picture framer will be able to advise you on suitable frames which will enhance your work.

Alphabets

Stitches

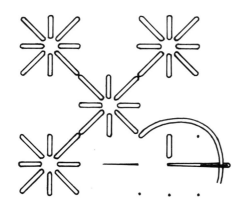

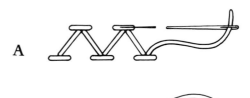

A

B

Chevron stitch

Algerian eye stitch

Back stitch

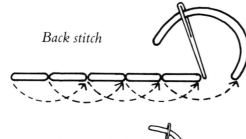

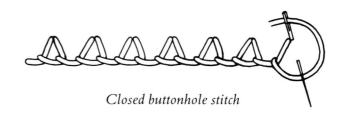

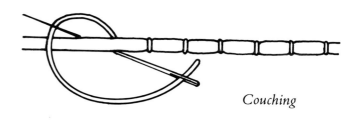

Closed buttonhole stitch

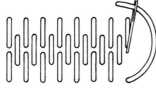

Brick stitch

Couching

Bullion knot or bar

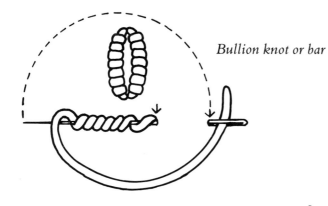

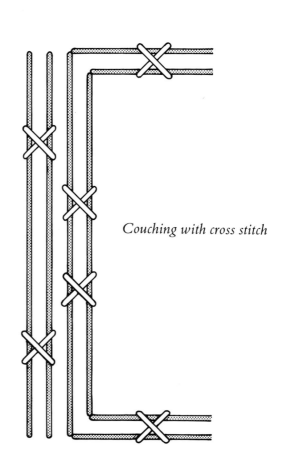

Couching with cross stitch

Buttonhole stitch

Chain stitch

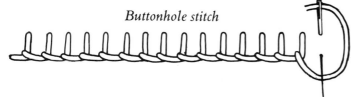

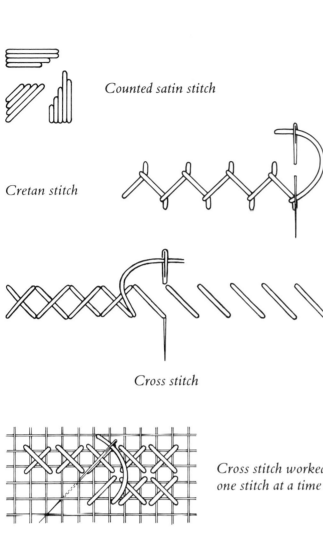

Counted satin stitch

Cretan stitch

Cross stitch

Cross stitch worked
one stitch at a time

Detached chain or lazy daisy stitch

Detached overcast stitch

Diagonal leaf stitch

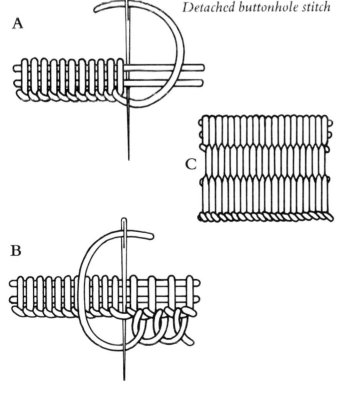

A

Detached buttonhole stitch

C

B

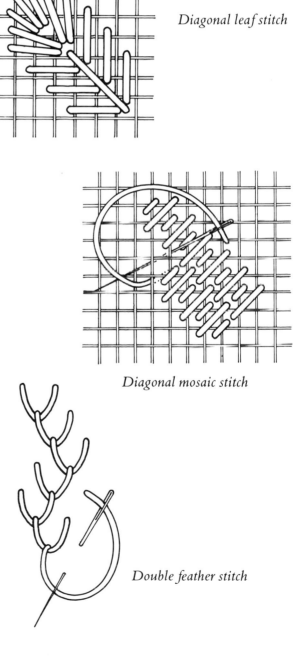

Diagonal mosaic stitch

Double feather stitch

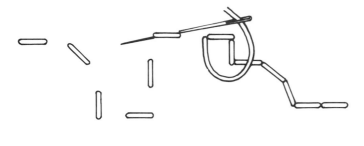

Double running or Holbein stitch

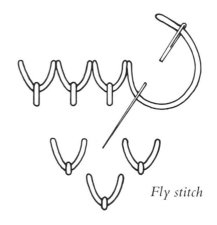

Fly stitch

Elongated cushion stitch

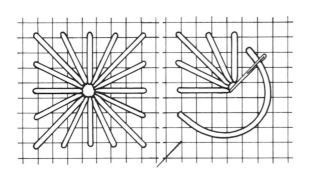

Eyelet stitch

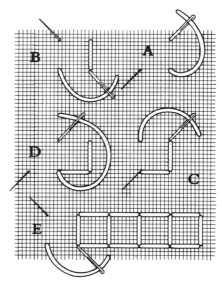

Four-sided stitch

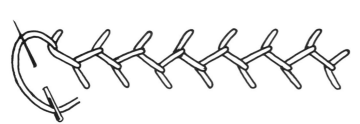

Feather stitch

French knot

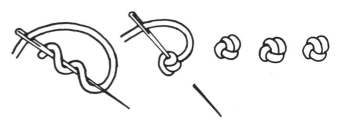

French knot with two twists

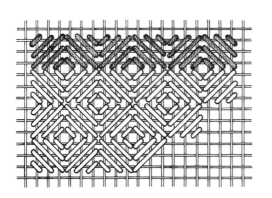

Flat stitch

Herringbone stitch

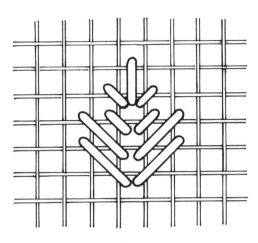

Leaf stitch

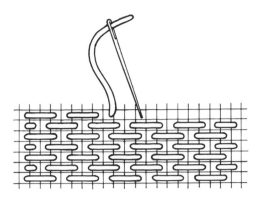

Pattern darning

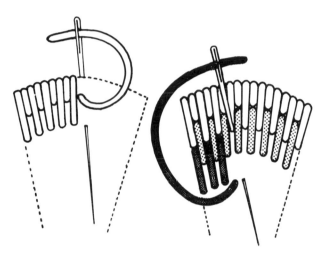

Long and short stitch

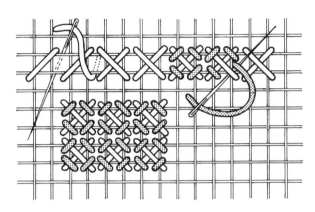

Rice stitch

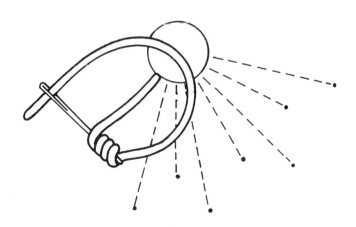

Long-legged French knot

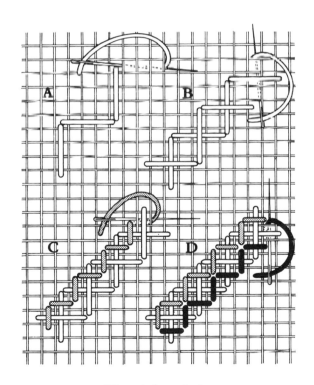

Rice stitch variation

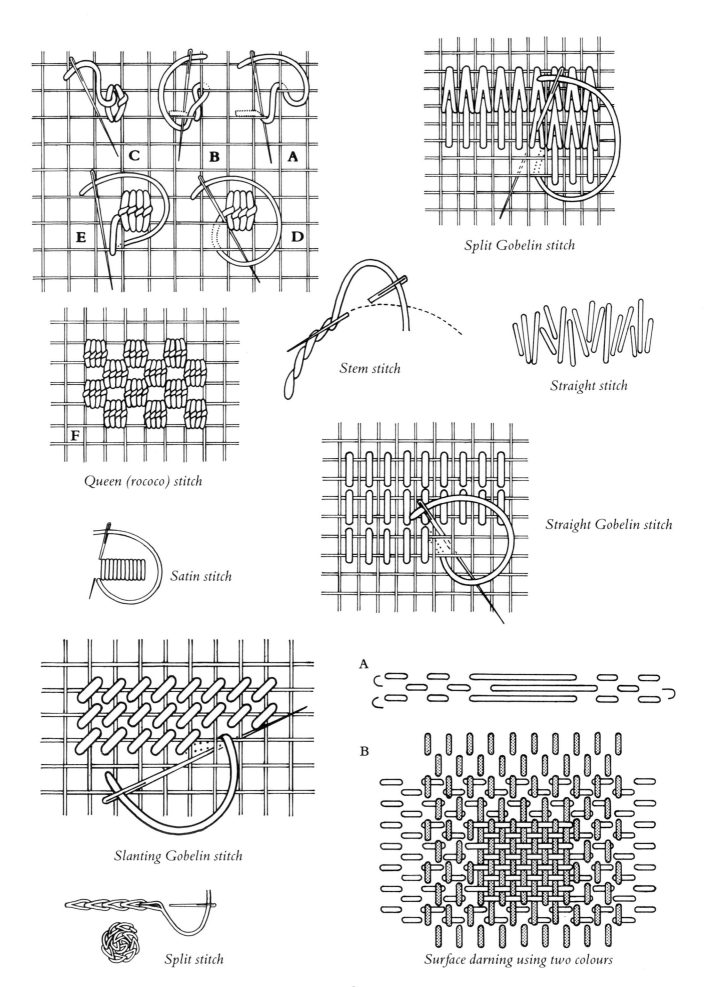

Split Gobelin stitch

Stem stitch

Straight stitch

Queen (rococo) stitch

Satin stitch

Straight Gobelin stitch

Slanting Gobelin stitch

Split stitch

Surface darning using two colours

*Tent stitch
(top) worked horizontally
(bottom) worked diagonally*

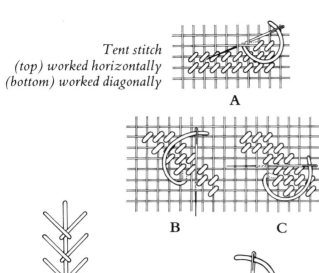

A

B   **C**

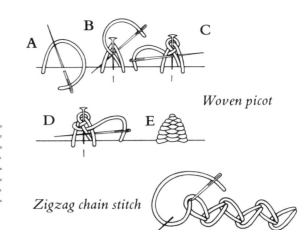

A   **B**   **C**

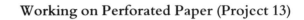

D   **E**

Woven picot

Thorn stitch

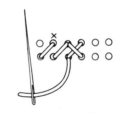

Two-way buttonhole stitch

Zigzag chain stitch

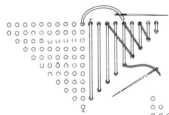

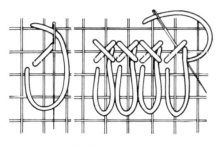

Velvet stitch

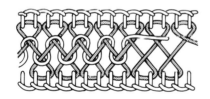

Threaded and laced buttonhole stitch

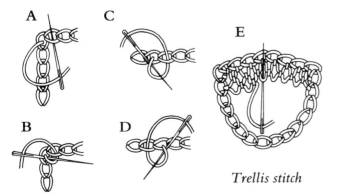

A   **C**   **E**

B   **D**

Trellis stitch

Working on Perforated Paper (Project 13)

*Working long stitches
on perforated paper*

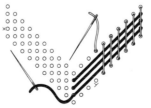

*Working the small stitches
on the triangles*

*Working fine diagonal
stitches over heavier
vertical stitches on top
and bottom triangles*

*Working fine diagonal
stitches over heavier
vertical stitches on
V-shapes*

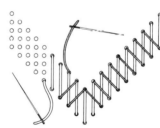

*Working vertical stitches
on top of long diagonal
stitches*

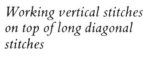

*Working fine horizontal
stitches over heavier
vertical stitches*

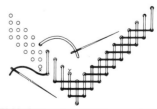

THREAD CONVERSION CHART

For DMC, Anchor and Madeira stranded embroidery cotton (floss), and DMC and Anchor pearl cotton and coton à broder. If no equivalent is given, use the nearest colour available. The colour illustration of the project will help you.

DMC	ANCHOR	MADEIRA
White/neige	01	White
Ecru	0387	Ecru
057	1203	–
067	–	–
094	1216	–
104	–	–
223	0895	0812
304	047	0509
310 (Black)	0403	Black
312	0979	1005
315	0970	0810
316	0969	0809
317	0400	1714
320	0215	1311
327	0101	0805
334	0977	1003
347	019	0407
352	09	0303
353	08	0304
355	5968	0401
356	5975	0402
394	013	0212
414	0399	1801
415	0398	1803
422	0367	2102
436	0363	2011
437	0362	2012
444	0291	0106
470	0266	1502
471	0265	1501
498	047	0511
500	0879	1705
517	0171	1107
520	–	–

DMC	ANCHOR	MADEIRA
523	–	–
524	–	–
550	0101	0714
552	0100	0713
553	098	0712
554	096	0711
564	–	–
580	0268	1608
581	0280	1609
598	0928	1111
603	076	0701
606	0335	0209
608	0332	0206
610	0905	2106
611	0889	2107
612	0898	2108
640	0393	1905
644	0391	1907
666	046	0210
676	0891	2208
677	0886	2207
700	0230	1304
703	0239	1307
704	0238	1308
712	0926	2101
718	088	0707
720	–	–
727	0293	0109
729	0890	2209
733	–	1611
738	0361	2013
742	0303	0114
743	0305	0113
744	0301	0112

DMC	ANCHOR	MADEIRA
762	0397	1804
776	025	0503
778	0968	0808
780	0309	2214
792	0941	0905
793	0121	0906
796	0133	0913
799	0130	0910
801	0359	2007
828	0158	1101
831	0906	2201
832	0907	2202
839	0380	1913
842	0376	1910
844	0401	1810
890	0218	1314
902	072	0601
905	0257	1412
906	0256	1411
907	0255	1410
917	089	0706
920	0339	0312
924	0851	1706
927	0848	1708
930	0922	1712
935	0269	1505
936	0846	1507
937	0268	1504
943	0188	1203
947	0925	0205
948	0933	0306
950	4146	2309
951	0880	2308
963	048	0608
972	0298	0107
986	0246	1404
991	0212	1204
992	0187	1202
995	0410	1102
996	0433	1103
–	0369	–
–	0858	–
–	0859	–
3022	0393	1903
3031	0360	2003
3032	0903	2002
3042	0870	0807
3052	0861	1509

DMC	ANCHOR	MADEIRA
3346	0267	1407
3347	0266	1408
3348	0265	1409
3350	078	0603
3354	075	0606
3362	–	–
3685	070	0602
3712	–	–
3713	–	–
3716	–	–
3731	–	–
3733	–	–
3740	–	–
3750	–	–
3765	–	–
3772	–	–
–	0279	–
–	0185	–

PROJECT 12 *COLOUR AND PATTERN* and PROJECT 13 *SAMPLER GREETINGS CARD:*

The equivalent of 20th Century Yarns Fine Silk is four strands of stranded embroidery cotton (floss) to one of silk. The nearest colour equivalents are:

Amethyst	DMC 550
Damson	DMC 95
Flamingo	DMC 51
Nutmeg	DMC 69
Pacific	Madeira 1204
Poppy	DMC 99
Sorcery	DMC 310

Madeira Stranded Embroidery Cotton (floss) may be used in place of Au Ver à Soie Stranded Silk. The nearest colour equivalents are:

AU VER A SOIE	MADEIRA
115	1102
134	1203
946	0513
1034	0703
1335	0903

BIBLIOGRAPHY

◆

Historical Background

Ashton, Leigh. *Samplers* (Medici Society 1926)
Clabburn, Pamela. *Samplers* (Shire Publications 1977), *The Needleworker's Dictionary* (Macmillan 1976)
Colby, Averil. *Samplers* (Batsford 1964, 1984)
Edmonds, Mary Jaene. *Samplers and Samplermakers – An American Schoolgirl Art* (Charles Letts 1991)
Fawdry, Marguerite and Brown, Deborah. *The Book of Samplers* (Lutterworth Press 1980)
Garrad, Larch S. and Hayhurst, Yvonne M. *Samplers in the Collection of the Manx Museum* (Manx Museum and National Trust 1988)
King, Donald. *Samplers* (Her Majesty's Stationery Office 1960)
Morris, Barbara. *Victorian Embroidery* (Herbert Jenkins 1962)
Sayer, Chloe. *Mexican Textiles* (British Museum Publications 1990)

Sebba, Anne. *Samplers, Five Centuries of a Gentle Craft* (Weidenfeld and Nicolson 1979)
Walton, Karin M. *Samplers in the City of Bristol Museum and Art Gallery* (City of Bristol Museum and Art Gallery 1983)
Embroidered Samplers in the Collection of the Cooper-Hewitt Museum (The Smithsonian Institute's National Museum of Design 1984)

Basic Techniques

Christie, Mrs Archibald. *Samplers and Stitches* (Batsford 1989)
Coleman, Anne. *The Creative Sewing Machine* (Batsford 1979)
Rivers, Margaret. *Working on Canvas* (Batsford 1990)
Swift, Gay. *Machine Stitchery* (Batsford 1974)
Mary Thomas's Embroidery Book (Hodder & Stoughton 1936)

SUPPLIERS

◆

Embroidery shops, craft shops and some department stores:
Beads, Bondaweb, canvas, cords, embroidery frames, fabrics (including silk noil), felt, gold net, indelible markers, needles, ribbons (including metallic ribbons), sequins, sequin waste, threads, vilene (pellon)

Craft and model shops:
Humbrol mini spray paint

Craft shops:
Bondaweb, fabric paints and dyes, indelible markers, perforated paper, PVA adhesive, shisha mirrors

Stationers and art materials shops:
Tissue paper, tracing paper

Art materials or graphic supplies shops:
Acrylic paints, mounting card, permanent drawing pens

If you have difficulty in finding any of the materials listed for the samplers, the specialist suppliers listed below may be able to help you. Other addresses can be found in embroidery and craft magazines:

2oth Century Yarns
The Red House
Guilsborough
Northants NN6 9PU
Tel: (0604) 740348
Variegated Fine Silk
(Mail order only)

Campden Needlecraft Centre
High Street
Chipping Campden
Glos
Tel: (0386) 840583
Specialist embroidery threads and fabrics, including Au Ver à Soie stranded silk
(Shop and mail order)

Jane Greenoff's Inglestone Collection
Inglestone
Milton Place
Fairford
Glos GL7 4HR
Tel: (0285) 712778
Perforated paper

Shades at Mace & Nairn
89 Crane Street
Salisbury
Wilts SP1 2PY
Tel: (0722) 336903
Embroidery specialists, including Deka fabric paints and transfer dyes
(Shop and mail order)

Barnyarns
Langrish
Petersfield
Hants GU32 1RQ
Tel: (0730) 267201
Embroidery specialists
(Mail order only)

The Silk Route
32 Wolseley Road
Godalming
Surrey GU7 3EA
Metallic silk organza
(Mail order only)

Steff Francis
South Cottage
Hookley Lane
Elstead
Godalming
Surrey GU8 6JB
Tel: (02522) 703222
Hand-dyed silk threads and viscose ribbon

Mulberry Silks
Number 2 Old Rectory Cottage
Easton Grey
Malmesbury
Wilts SN16 0PE
Tel: (0666) 840881
(Mail order only)

Silken Strands
33 Linksway
Gatley
Cheadle
Cheshire SK8 4LA
Tel: 061-428 9108
Shisha mirrors, beads
(Mail order, callers by appointment)

ACKNOWLEDGEMENTS

◊

Photographs from the Embroiderers' Guild Collection

The Embroiderers' Guild would like to thank all those who contributed to this book: Julia Hedgecoe and Dudley Moss (photography), Mollie Picken (technical diagrams), Margaret Rivers (co-ordinator), Lynn Szygenda (Curator of the Embroiderers' Guild Collection) and the embroiderers who designed and worked the contemporary samplers: Lesley Barnett, Muriel Best, Jenny Bullen, Rosemary Caie, Marion Glover, Jane Greenoff, Janice Hay, Mary Jenkins, Brenda Keyes, Vicky Lugg, Moyra McNeill, Sheila Miller, Jennie Parry, Patricia Sales, Willemien Stevens, Jo Verso, Pamela Warner.

The following information applies to the historical samplers from the Embroiderers' Guild Collection. The reference numbers are the museum code numbers.

page 5, EG23 – 1987, 250 x 910mm (9¾ x 35½in) Given by Miss Hester Clough; page 7, EG 1433, 150 x 255mm (6 x 10in), Given by the Needlework Development Scheme, Photograph by Julia Hedgecoe; page 8, EG79 – 1982, 225 x 425mm (8¾ x 16½in), Given by the Needlework Development Scheme, Photograph by Julia Hedgecoe; page 9, EG7 – 1982, 160 x 510mm (6¼ x 20in); pages 10–11, EG48 – 1987, 280 x 380mm (11 x 15in), Given by Miss Hester Clough; page 13, EG15 – 1990, 225 x 315mm (8⅞ x 12in); page 15, EG 3530, 290 x 240mm (11 x 9½in); page 17, EG78 – 1982, 230 x 780mm (9 x 3¾in); pages 23, 24, 25, EG29 –

1987, 210 x 750mm (8¼ x 29½in), Given by Miss Hester Clough; page 33, EG25 – 1987, 230 x 350mm (9 x 13½), Given by Miss Hester Clough; pages 38–39, EG51 – 1987, 250 x 350mm (9¾ x 13⅞in); page 45, EG 2091, 320 x 410mm (12⅝ x 16¼in), Given by Miss Henwood, Photograph by Julia Hedgecoe; pages 51–53, EG 4785, 405 x 320mm (16½ x 12½in); page 59, EG14 – 1990, 330 x 340mm (13 x 13¼in), Photograph by Julia Hedgecoe; page 65, EG18 – 1992, 490 x 580mm (19⅜ x 22⅞in); pages 74–75, 77, 78, EG 943, 330 x 330mm (13 x 13in), Given by the Needlework Development Scheme; page 83, EG

1746, 120 x 1460mm (4¾ x 57½in), Given by Essie Newberry; page 83, EG 3148, 180 x 1100mm (7 x 43⅜in), Given by Mrs D. Cooper; pages 94–95, EG19 – 1992, 110 x 190mm (4⁵/₁₀ x 7½in); pages 98–99, 100, 101, EG 3061, 480 x 480mm (19 x 19in), Given by Miss M. I. Young; pages 107, 111, EG25 – 1988, 143 x 143mm (56½ x 56½in), Given by Mrs Winifred Smith; page 113, EG20 – 1992, 115 x 235mm (4⁹/₁₀ x 9¼in); page 119, EG 4735, 140 x 450mm (5½ x 17¾in), Given by Miss K. Alldworth; pages 124–125, 126, EG 2719, 470 x 470mm (18 x 18in), Given by the Hon. Rachel Gordon.

INDEX

40-498-3